SOCIAL
RESEARCH ON
CHILDREN AND
ADOLESCENTS

OTHER RECENT VOLUMES IN THE
SAGE FOCUS EDITIONS

SOCIAL RESEARCH ON CHILDREN AND ADOLESCENTS

Ethical Issues

Barbara Stanley
Joan E. Sieber
editors

SAGE PUBLICATIONS
The International Professional Publishers
Newbury Park   London   New Delhi

Copyright © 1992 by Sage Publications, Inc.

For information address:

SAGE Publications, Inc.
2455 Teller Road
Newbury Park, California 91320

SAGE Publications Ltd.
6 Bonhill Street
London EC2A 4PU
United Kingdom

SAGE Publications India Pvt. Ltd.
M-32 Market
Greater Kailash I
New Delhi 110 048 India

Printed in the United States of America

Library of Congress Cataloging-in-Publication Data

Main entry under title:

Social research on children and adolescents: Ethical issues / Barbara Stanley
and Joan E. Sieber, Editors.
    p.   cm.—(Sage focus editions)
    Includes bibliographical references and indexes.
    ISBN 0-8039-4333-4.—ISBN 0-8039-4334-2 (pbk.)
    1. Children—Research—United States. 2. Teenagers—Research—
United States. I. Stanley, Barbara, 1949- . II. Sieber, Joan E.
III. National Institutes of Health (U.S.). Office for
Protection from Research Risk.
HQ767.85.E84   1992   91-13620
305.23'072073—dc20   CIP

FIRST PRINTING, 1992

Sage Production Editor: Judith L. Hunter

Contents

Part II: The Consent Process

Part III: Research on High-Risk Behavior

1

Introduction

The Ethics of Social Research
on Children and Adolescents

BARBARA STANLEY
JOAN E. SIEBER

Increasingly, the applied social scientist is directed by national priorities and funding sources to study social problems involving young
people. Much applied social research on children and adolescents focuses on such high-risk events as physical and sexual abuse, depression and suicidal tendencies, running away from home, gang
behavior, substance abuse, teenage pregnancy, and exposure to AIDS.
Even while studying youngsters in the context of family, school, or
institutional life when the *intended focus* of the research seems innocuous, it is not unusual for the investigator to happen upon high-risk
behavior. For example, in the course of research on the social development of latchkey children, the outcome of joint custody arrangements, or the social development of disabled children, it is not
unusual to find in one's sample some youngsters who are being sexually abused, who are using drugs, or who think they may have AIDS.
Current societal problems and the funding priorities these dictate
leave the investigator little opportunity to avoid studying or encountering these problems. Yet the legal, ethical, and practical constraints
governing research on minors seem, on the face of it, to place the investigator in an impossible position.

Young people, especially adolescents, are likely to engage in rebellious behavior designed to separate themselves from their parents. Much of the high-risk behavior of adolescents occurs without parental knowledge. Yet, adolescents may not participate in research without approval of a parent or guardian, except as set forth in federal law, 46.408(c), subpart D of 48 FR 9818, March 8, 1983. (46.408(c) appears on page 28, in the Appendix to chapter 2.) Runaways may qualify to be studied without parental consent, but what happens if they decide to return home? May the researcher continue to collect data without parental consent? Is the researcher ever obligated to disclose anything about the research findings to the parents?

In Western society, the youth culture increasingly takes on a life of its own in which its members consider themselves to have the rights and privileges of adults. In fact, children and adolescents are on their way to becoming autonomous adults. Their increasing capacity to decide for themselves and to keep parts of their life private from intrusion from others should be respected. But what are the implications of these developmental changes for the researcher who is constrained to seek parental permission for the youngster's research participation, as well as the informed assent of the youngster? For example, what are the obligations of the scientist who learns, in the course of the research, of secrets that the youngster keeps from the parents, to the youngster's detriment?

It may appear that the ethical codes and laws that govern research are ill-designed—that research could proceed more satisfactorily without them. On closer examination, it is apparent that these codes and laws protect important interests. It is *conflicts among these interests* that create dilemmas for the researcher. For example, conflicts arise between the interests of adolescents in having autonomy and privacy, and the interests of parents in exercising some control over their children. Of necessity, the researcher must find somehow a way to respect both sets of interests.

The purpose of this interdisciplinary book is to examine the manifold dilemmas that may confront investigators who seek to do research on children and adolescents, and to provide practical approaches to solving those problems. It bridges some of the gaps between the legal requirements that govern research on minors, what we know about the psychology of children and adolescents, and the scientific requirements of research. It begins with an examination of the federal and state laws that govern research on children and adolescents. The succeeding chapters examine the ways in which these laws are interpreted and applied in research on youngsters. Several main issues are woven throughout these chapters.

- How are we to understand the rights and r eeds of children in relation to legal and psychological concepts?
- Although the law might seem to suggest that a quantum leap is taken from childhood to adulthood, both psychology and the law rc cognize that this is not so. What are the implications for research procedures of the youngster's gradual psychological development into adulthood? How does the law take these psychological factors into account in the regulation of research on youngsters? How should investigators take these psychological factors into account in designing research procedures?
- When are parents unlikely to decide in the best interests of their children, and how does this influence the consent process? The researcher must strike a balance between respecting the rights of parents and protecting the interests of youngsters. How does one decide who should consent in the case of children who are being abused or neglected by their parents, parents who are incompetent, runaway children, children who are identified as incorrigible, children in the custody of hospitals or other institutions, or children who might be considered "mature minors"?
- Although minors usually cannot give legal consent to participate in research, at least their "assent" to participate should be obtained. That is, after the parent or guardian's permission for the child's research participation is obtained, an appropriate consent procedure should then be carried out with the youngster. What should be included in such consent or assent statements, depending on the population, the research setting and risks, the developmental stage of the youngster, and the degree of parental guidance?
- How does one evaluate research risk and benefit in relation to the psychological development of research participants? Risk is relative to the vulnerabilities of the individual, and benefit is relative to the ability of the individual to profit from a given experience. What are the relevant lessons from developmental psychology? What are the implications of the status of children vis-à-vis adults, of children's limited range of experience, or of their immature cognitive processes for the consequences of their participation in a given research activity?

With respect to these and many of the other issues examined here, no simple generalizations can be made across research settings, across the developmental span, or across kinds of children. Rather, this book points to factors that make a difference and opens the discussions that should occur as researchers seek to develop valid and respectful procedures for research on children and adolescents.

The need for such discussion is acute. Although social scientists are expected to address sensitive social problems of children and adolescents, the traditional tools of the social sciences do not equip them to bridge the gap between the requirements of research rigor on the one hand, and legal and ethical requirements on the other. Those who have not done community-based or applied research on youngsters may be tempted to regard the problem as one caused by bad laws or misguided "ethics." Some laws are indeed imperfect, but even well-formulated laws are, by their very nature, likely to try the patience and challenge the creativity of researchers. Laws governing research on humans are grounded in the principles of ethics and decency under which people expect, or at least hope, to live. For example, parents expect to have a say about what happens to their children, and both parents and children want their privacy respected. The researcher-as-parent may favor such laws. But the researcher-as-researcher does not enjoy spending precious research resources and enduring the attrition of a carefully selected sample in the process of obtaining consent, especially from parents who may disrespect or misunderstand science. Researchers need only ask themselves what wrath they would unleash on a stranger who tried to usurp their parental role in order to understand that the law stands between two potentially destructive parties, preserving order and dignity as best it can.

Many of those now engaged in applied research on minors were trained in more traditional laboratory settings and have little sense of how to integrate the requirements of research rigor and compliance with current laws that specify the rights of research participants. Even those trained recently are unlikely to have answers to the following problems, some solutions to which are presented in chapters of this book as indicated.

1. What legal constraints exist concerning research on children? (Areen, chapter 2)
2. What do the relevant federal regulations of research actually say? (An Appendix to chapter 2 contains the relevant federal regulations.)
3. What do theory and research on human development indicate about youngsters' vulnerability to various kinds of research risk and how vulnerability may be reduced? (Thompson, chapter 3)
4. By the beginning of middle childhood, children manifest an interest in having private space, as evidenced by the KEEP OUT signs that often appear on children's bedroom doors. By adolescence, most youngsters wish to exercise considerable control over the access that others have to information about them. What does the law say about youngsters' rights to privacy? What are implications for research? (Melton, chapter 4)

5. Ethical theory intended to guide research on humans, as formulated by the National Commission on the Protection of Human Subjects in Biomedical and Behavioral Research, is largely silent on how researchers should respect the privacy and autonomy of youngsters who are in the process of becoming adults. Yet the literature of developmental psychology demonstrates that early in adolescence most youngsters have adult-like decision-making abilities. How should the relevant ethical theory or guidelines be applied to minors as they approach adulthood? (Macklin, chapter 5)

6. Under what circumstances is parent or guardian consent not an appropriate mechanism for protecting the rights and interests of children who participate in research? (Grisso, chapter 6)

7. How does one explain research participation to youngsters? How can current knowledge of children's cognitive processes be used to improve the assent process? When is one a "mature minor" so situated to give legal consent? (Tymchuk, chapter 7)

8. Various laws require that researchers disclose dangerous acts of minors to their parents or others. How does one define a "dangerous act" with respect to minors whose whole life-style is dangerous (e.g., cocaine users who are sharing needles and engaging in violent behavior)? When is disclosure appropriate? (Rotheram-Borus & Koopman, chapter 8)

9. Community intervention research on minors may involve a wide range of interests and inputs—scientific, political, law enforcement, legal, financial. When interventions depend on the support of many sectors of the community, they also may become the focus of competing interests and demands, some of which may be at odds with legal, scientific, and ethical requirements of research on minors. How may these problems arise when the scientist is in charge, versus when the scientist is simply called in afterward to evaluate the program? What are the responsibilities of the scientist in each case? (Sieber, chapter 9)

10. What issues should one consider when evaluating the ethics and legality, as well as the psychological appropriateness, of a given proposal for research on minors? A summary of such issues is presented in the Epilogue. This summary is not intended to be read or used apart from the preceding chapters, which provide the context and detail that render the issues understandable. (Epilogue, a summary of the issues discussed in the private and public meetings of the Task Force on Research on Minors)

Each high-risk research setting tends to pose some unique ethical, legal, and procedural problems and must be evaluated on its own. A common thread of problems runs through these research settings, and it is possible—and essential—that investigators learn from one another.

The authors of the succeeding chapters explore a wide range of the problems that confront the social and behavioral researcher who studies minors. They focus primarily on research settings in which parental consent is probably not feasible—research on runaway teenagers, incarcerated youth, pregnant teenagers, gay teenagers at risk of AIDS whose parents are not aware of their sexual orientation. Each chapter raises a host of ethical and methodological problems and then uses concepts from ethics, developmental psychology, and research methodology to examine the issues raised. Each develops criteria for selecting scientifically and ethically acceptable solutions that the investigator can live with and that satisfy legal and social perceptions of the rights of minor research participants and their parents or guardians.

The topics discussed in this book will interest the advanced undergraduate, graduate student, or senior investigator who wishes to do social or behavioral research on children and adolescents. It will also interest research administrators and human subjects review committees who bear institutional responsibility for the ethics and legality of research that is conducted under their purview. The chapters may be read usefully at two levels: by the nonscientist who wants an overview of the practical, ethical, and legal difficulties of conducting research on youngsters, and by the social scientist who wishes to build on extensive knowledge of human development, research methodology, and practical problems of research on children or adolescents.

This book is the work of a task force on research on minors that was organized by the Office for Protection from Research Risk of the National Institutes of Health. These chapters have been the focus of meetings and workshops, where they have been received favorably by various audiences of social scientists and research administrators. We gratefully acknowledge the participation of those who attended the meetings, those who prepared the papers that became chapters of this book, and David Yamamoto, a student at California State University, Hayward, who prepared the author and subject indexes.

Reference

48 Federal Regulation 9818, 46.408 (c), subpart D (March 8, 1983).

2

Legal Constraints on Social Research
With Children

JUDITH AREEN

Introduction

Debate has long raged about when, if ever, it is ethical to conduct nontherapeutic research on children. Paul Ramsey argued, for example, that the use of a nonconsenting subject such as a child is wrong whether or not there is any risk posed to the subject (Ramsey, 1970, p. 17) By contrast, Richard McCormick supports such research, but only if it involves no discernible risk to the children (McCormick, 1974).[1]

In 1983, attempting to strike a balance between these two positions, the Department of Health and Human Services adopted federal regulations to govern behavioral research on children. The regulations require that an institutional review board (IRB) approve proposed research and obtain both the consent of the parents and the assent of the child. The regulations also permit the IRB to waive the parental consent requirement, although it may be necessary to establish an appropriate substitute.

The waiver provision does not exempt the research from the requirements of state or federal law. The common law in force in most states requires parental consent for important decisions involving minors until they are emancipated.[2]

This chapter examines the pertinent federal regulations and compares them with relevant state law. It concludes that the federal

7

regulations are likely to be more a source of assistance than a hindrance to researchers in meeting the requirements of law. Approaches to clarifying the mandates of state and federal law are discussed.

Federal Regulations

Regulations for the Protection of Human Subjects

Federal regulations governing research involving human subjects and conducted or funded by the National Institutes of Health were first adopted in 1974.[3] All research subject to the regulations must be approved in advance by an IRB that has determined whether, among other things, the risk to subjects is reasonable in relation to anticipated benefits, the selection of subjects is equitable, and informed consent will be obtained from each prospective subject or the subject's legally authorized representative (45 C.F.R. 46.111, 1983).

The regulations apply to behavioral, as well as biomedical, research (45 C.F.R. 46.101 and 102[f]). A 1981 revision of the regulations implicitly acknowledged that a difference exists between the two types of research, however, by exempting from the regulatory process most survey or interview research and most observational studies in public settings. Survey research remains subject to the IRB process only when information about sensitive matters is collected in such a manner that the subjects could be identified and their responses could expose them to civil or criminal liability or be damaging to their financial standing or employability (45 C.F.R. 46.101).

Additional Regulations for Research Involving Children

In 1983 additional regulations were adopted to govern research involving children (48 Fed. Reg. 9814, 1983). In general, the federal regulations permit research involving children (including survey and interview research), provided that the parents consent and the child assents and the research involves only "minimal risk."

Unfortunately, the definition provided for "minimal risk" is not very informative. The regulations merely provide that "minimal risk" means that the risks of harm anticipated in the proposed research are not greater, "considering probability and magnitude, than those ordinarily encountered in daily life or during the performance of routine physical or psychological examinations or tests" (45 C.F.R. 46.102[g]). Assent is defined as "a child's affirmative agreement to participate in research." Because children are intimidated easily and might be afraid to object, the regulations provide that "[m]ere failure to object should not, absent affirmative agreement, be construed as assent" (45 C.F.R. 46.402).

The Department of Health and Human Services did suggest that, if the research involves risk, then it should be conducted first on adults "in order to ascertain the degree of risk" (48 Fed. Reg. 9816, 1983). If that is not relevant or possible, research is to be conducted on older children before progressing to younger children (48 Fed. Reg. 9816).

Research involving "greater than minimal risk" that also presents the prospect of direct benefit to the individual subjects may be conducted, but only if the risk is justified by the anticipated benefit and no reasonable alternatives present less risk.

Research that involves a minor increase over minimal risk and no prospect of direct benefit to the individual child subject may be conducted, but only if

1. The intervention or procedure presents experiences to subjects that are reasonably commensurate with those inherent in their actual or expected medical, dental, psychological, social or educational situations;
2. The intervention or procedure is likely to yield generalizable knowledge about the subjects' disorder or condition which is of vital importance for the understanding or amelioration of the subjects' disorder or condition; and
3. Adequate provisions are made for soliciting assent of the children and permission of their parents or guardians. (45 C.F.R. 46.406)

Unfortunately, no illustrations of what constitutes a "minor increase over minimal risk" are provided in the regulations.

Finally, research involving more than a minor increase over minimal risk and no prospect of direct benefit may be conducted, but only if the research is approved by a panel of experts appointed by the secretary of the Department of Health and Human Services (DHHS; 45 C.F.R. 46.407)

Provisions for Waiving Consent

The requirement of parental or guardian consent may be waived by the IRB in two circumstances. First, consent may be waived if (a) it involves only minimal risk to the subjects, (b) it will not affect adversely the rights or welfare of the subjects, and (c) the research could not practically be carried out without the waiver (45 C.F.R. 46.116; 45 C.F.R. 46.408[c]). Second, consent may be waived if it will not operate to protect the child (45 C.F.R. 46.408[c]). The regulations specifically mention research involving neglected or abused children as an example of a situation in which it would be permissible to waive the requirement of parental or guardian consent.

If parental or guardian permission is waived, an appropriate mechanism for protecting the children who will participate as subjects in the research must be substituted by the IRB (45 C.F.R. 46.408[c]). The requirement for assent by the child subject may be waived for similar reasons, or if "the capability of some or all of the children is so limited that they cannot reasonably be consulted (45 C.F.R. 46.408[a]).

Unfortunately, the regulations provide little guidance about the establishment of a substitute mechanism. They merely provide that "[t]he choice of an appropriate mechanism would depend upon the nature and purpose of the activities described in the protocol, the risk and anticipated benefit to the research subjects, and their age, maturity, status and condition" (45 C.F.R. 46.408[c]).

The report and recommendations issued by the National Commission for the Protection of Human Subjects of Biomedical and Behavioral Research (NCPHS, 1977) formed the basis for the regulations governing research on children ultimately adopted by the DHHS.[4] It is, therefore, a relevant although not necessarily authoritative source of additional information about the waiver procedure and about "appropriate" substitute mechanisms.

The commission report identifies four circumstances in which modification or waiver of the parental consent requirement might be appropriate:

1. Research designed to identify factors related to the incidence or treatment of certain conditions in adolescents for which, in certain jurisdictions, they legally may receive treatment without parental consent;
2. research in which the subjects are "mature minors" and the procedures involved entail essentially no more than minimal risk that such individuals might reasonably assume on their own;
3. research designed to understand and meet the needs of neglected or abused children, or children designated by their parents as "in need of supervision"; and

4. research involving children whose parents are legally or functionally incompetent. (NCPHS, 1977, p. 17)

On the subject of appropriate substitute mechanisms, the report provides in pertinent part:

> There is no single mechanism that can be substituted for parental permission in every instance. In some cases the consent of mature minors should be sufficient. In other cases court approval may be required. . . .
>
> Another alternative might be to appoint a social worker, pediatric nurse, or physician to act as surrogate parent when the research is designed, for example, to study neglected or battered children. Such surrogate parents would be expected to participate not only in the process of soliciting the children's cooperation but also in the conduct of the research in order to provide reassurance for the subjects and to intervene or support their desires to withdraw if participation becomes too stressful. (43 Fed. Reg. 2084, 1978)

In summary, the regulations permit IRB's to waive consent requirements. The waiver standards are broadest when the research involves no more than minimal risk to the subjects. If more risk is involved, then the more restrictive provisions of Sec. 46.408 apply. The IRB must find that the requirement of parental permission is "not reasonable" and must provide an appropriate substitute mechanism.

State Law

The federal regulations provide that an IRB may waive the requirement of parental or guardian permission only if "the waiver is not inconsistent with federal, state or local law" (45 C.F.R. 46.116[e]; 45 C.F.R. 46.408[c]). Because the federal waiver provisions do not preempt state law requirements, it is necessary to examine the requirements established by state law in some detail.[5]

The common law, which forms the background for most state law on this subject, does not authorize minors to make important decisions without parental consent until they are emancipated.[6] States are free to depart from the common law standards, of course, either by court decision or by enacting statutes granting authority for particular decisions to minors. Most states, for example, have enacted statutes that authorize minors to consent to at least some medical treatments without parental consent or even notification. (These statutes typically authorize minors to consent to treatment for venereal disease or, in some states, psychotherapy.)

By tradition, statutes that alter the common law are construed narrowly. Therefore, in the absence of a state statute explicitly authorizing minors to consent to research, such authority probably cannot be presumed merely because a state statute authorizes minors to obtain particular medical treatments without parental consent.

Behavioral research generally is less likely than biomedical research to result in an injury to a subject. Nonetheless, if behavioral research presents a foreseeable risk to a subject (that the subject might be injured emotionally as a result of participation in the research, for example), and such injury does occur, the researcher might be found liable. That is, an injured subject might be found entitled to compensation if proof existed that the researcher negligently failed to avoid the injury.

The uncertain legal status of research involving children reflects the fact that few court decisions exist in the field. In *Neilson v. Regents of the University of California* (1973), the proceedings were dismissed for lack of prosecution when the plaintiff did not pursue the matter, so no light was shed on the legal status of research involving children (Holder, 1985, p. 152). The research at issue in *Neilson* was a study of the development of allergic disease in infants and children born in families with a history of allergies. The proposed protocol included a number of invasive techniques. Families who participated were to be paid approximately $300 a year. A lawyer who was a member of the institution review board of the university in which the research was proposed sought to enjoin the research on the ground that the parent of a minor child does not have the legal right to subject a child to procedures not intended for the child's benefit.

Cases do exist in which a subject (or the parent of a subject) has brought an action for invasion of privacy after damaging information about the subject was released inappropriately. In *Doe v. McMillan* (1977), the United States Court of Appeals for the District of Columbia Circuit was faced with the issue of whether the publication and distribution of a congressional report that allegedly identified school children in a derogatory manner violated the children's right to privacy. The court held that no violation existed because of constitutional immunity provided to members of Congress, but implicit in this opinion is authority for the conclusion that private researchers could be held liable for using such information without parental consent.

Conclusion

On balance, the federal regulations are likely to be more a source of assistance than a hindrance to behavioral researchers. By identifying categories of low-risk research for which no IRB review is needed and by authorizing the waiver of parental consent in appropriate instances, the regulations generally will enable researchers to proceed with well-designed research. Researchers will be armed with the assurance, moreover, that if a legal challenge is brought against their work, their position should be strengthened by the fact that the research was approved in advance by a duly constituted IRB.

Although some state laws may conflict with the federal regulations, several approaches may be taken to minimize such conflict. First, the requirements of state law are almost certain to be satisfied if parental consent is obtained. It is only when a researcher wants to waive parental consent that state law requirements are likely to be more restrictive than the federal regulations.

Second, the statutes that authorize minors to obtain particular types of medical treatment without parental consent vary greatly in both scope and language. The language of at least some of these statutes may encompass authority for minors to consent to participation in behavioral research. Any researcher (or IRB) concerned about the legal constraints imposed by the law of the state in which the research is being conducted should discuss the matter directly with local counsel.

Third, researchers can and should make every effort to minimize the risk of harm or injury to subjects. In some studies, for example, it might be appropriate to debrief some or all of the subjects after data are collected from them. In others, it might be wise to screen participants to exclude subjects who would be particularly at risk for emotional injury.

Fourth, it is important to keep in mind that in most states the law is silent on the subject of the participation of minors in behavioral research. This silence is less of a barrier than if state law explicitly prohibited such participation. Fifth, because the federal regulations are arguably more protective of the interests of minors than the common law, if a legal challenge were brought to a particular protocol involving behavioral research with minors, a state court might be persuaded to uphold the protocol on the basis that state law is silent, so long as the research had been approved by an IRB and was consistent with the relevant federal regulations.

Finally, some commentators have argued that the same constitutional right of privacy that the Supreme Court has recognized entitles "mature" minors to obtain abortions without the knowledge or permission of their parents (*Bellotti v. Baird,* 1979) should also entitled mature minors to consent to participate in research (see, for example, Holder, 1988, p. 137). No court has yet ruled on this matter, however, so for the time being it is merely a theory about how courts might respond in the future.

The right to privacy claim for mature minors is somewhat hampered, moreover, by the fact that the Supreme Court did not provide a very clear definition of who is a "mature minor." The definition the Court set forth in *Bellotti v. Baird* (1979) has three parts. First, the determination of maturity must be made on a case-by-case basis, rather than by category. Thus, a state may not simply define all 17-year-olds as mature for purposes of exercising the constitutional right to abortion. Second, the Court held that a mature minor need not be economically independent of the parents, nor even emotionally or intellectually mature in all respects. In the Court's words, "the fact that a minor may be very much an adult in some respects does not mean that his need and opportunity for growth under parental guidance and discipline have ended" (*Bellotti v. Baird,* 1979). Third, the minor should be "mature enough and well enough informed to make her abortion decision, in consultation with her physician, independently of her parents' wishes" (*Bellotti v. Baird,* 1979).

A recent case in which a state court did extend the concept of mature minor beyond the reproductive context involved a 17-year-old with acute leukemia (*In re E.G.,* 1987). She and her parents had refused any blood transfusions because of their religious beliefs. The matter was litigated. On appeal, the court, citing *Bellotti,* stated that although the right of privacy has not been extended beyond reproductive matters, "we believe such an extension is inevitable" (*In re E.G.,* 1987, p. 290). The court also relied on an Illinois statute that provides that a minor 16 years of age or over who has demonstrated the capacity to manage his own affairs may be partially or completely emancipated.[6] The appellate court concluded that the 17-year-old should "be partially emancipated" and granted her the right to accept or refuse transfusions.[7]

An IRB that remains concerned about constraints that might be imposed by the law of the state in which it functions after having the matter analyzed by local counsel might seek either an advisory opinion from the state attorney general or a declaratory judgement from the local courts about the legality of a proposed protocol.

Notes

1. "To share in the general effort and burden of health maintenance and disease control is part of our flourishing and growth as humans. To the extent that it is a good for all of us to share this burden, we all ought to do so and to the extent that we *ught* to do so, it is a reasonable construction or presumption of our wishes to say that v e would do so. The reasonableness of this presumption validates vicarious consent. . . . Concretely, when a particular experiment would involve no discernible risks, no notable pain, no notable inconvenience, and yet holds promise of considerable benefit, should not the child be constructed to wish this in the way we presume he chooses his own life, because he *ought* to. I believe so." (McCormick, 1974, pp. 13-14)

2. The grounds for emancipation vary from state to state. In most, 18 is the age at which the legal disabilities of childhood end. At common law, marriage was also an emancipating event. A few states provide a statutory procedure by which children younger than 18 may be declared emancipated by a court. See, for example, Cal. Civ. Code Secs. 60-70 (West, 1982); Conn. Gen. Stat. Ann. Secs. 46b-150 to 150e (1986); Or. Rev. Stat. Secs. 109.555-565 (1989).

3. The federal regulations governing the protection of human subjects are set forth in 45 Code of Federal Regulations (CFR) 46. The regulations providing additional protections for children are in sections 46.401 to 46.409. The full text of the most pertinent regulations are set forth in the Appendix to this chapter as an aid to readers.

4. In 1974 Congress established the National Commission for the Protection of Human Subjects of Biomedical and Behavioral Research and directed the commission to make recommendations regarding the protection of human subjects in research. Congress provided that as part of its work, "The Commission shall identify the requirements for informed consent to participation in biomedical and behavioral research by children" (Public Law 93-348, 1974).

5. Although no federal laws exist directly on point, the Family Educational and Privacy Act (FERPA) requires that parental consent be obtained for the release of the education records of minor children (20 U.S.C. 1232[g][1988]). Any research that relies on protected records needs to follow the FERPA standards. The act has no waiver provision, moreover.

6. Ill. Rev. Stat., ch. 37, para 105-2(d)(3)(1985).

7. The appellate court decision was affirmed on common law grounds. The Illinois Supreme Court declined to address the constitutional holding. In re E. G., 549 D. E. 2d 322 (Ill. 1989).

References

Bellotti v. Baird, 443 U. S. 622 (1979).

Cal. Civ. Code Secs. 60-70. (West 1982).

Conn. Gen. Stat. Ann. Secs. 46b-150 to 150e (1986).

Doe v. McMillan, 566 F. 2d 713 (1977).

Family Educational and Privacy Act (FERPA). 20 U. S. C. 1232 g (1988).

43 Fed. Reg. 2084. (1978).

45 Code of Federal Regulations (CFR) 46, sections 46.101 to 46.409 (1983).

48 Fed. Reg. 9814. (1983).

48 Fed. Reg. 9816 (1983).

48 Fed. Reg. 9818 (March 8, 1983).

Holder, A. (1985). *Legal issues in pediatrics and adolescent medicine* (2nd ed.). New Haven, CT: Yale University Press.

Holder, A. R. (1988). Constraints on experimentation: Protecting children to death. *Yale Law and Policy Review, 6,* 137-156.

Ill. Rev. Stat. Ch. 37, para. 105-2(d)(3)(1985).

In re E. G., 515 N.E.2d 286 (Ill. App. 1987), aff'd in part 549 NE 2d 322 (Ill. 1989).

McCormick, R. (1974). Proxy consent in the experimentation situation. *18 Perspectives in Biology and Medicine, 2,* 13-14.

National Commission for the Protection of Human Subjects of Biomedical and Behavioral Research (NCPHS). (1977). *Report and recommendations: Research involving children.* Washington, DC: Government Printing Office.

Neilsen v. Regents of the University of California, No. 665-047 (Sup. Ct. of Cal. 1973).

Or. Rev. Stat. Secs. 109.555-565.

Public Law 93-348. (1974).

Ramsey, P. (1970). *The patient as person.* New Haven, CT: Yale University Press.

Appendix:
Selected Federal Regulations for
the Protection of Human Subjects

§ 46.101 To what do these regulations apply?

(a) Except as provided in paragraph (b) of this section, this subpart applies to all research involving human subjects conducted by the Department of Health and Human Services or funded in whole or in part by a Department grant, contract, cooperative agreement or fellowship.

(1) This includes research conducted by Department employees, except each Principal Operating Component head may adopt such nonsubstantive, procedural modifications as may be appropriate from an administrative standpoint.

(2) It also includes research conducted or funded by the Department of Health and Human Services outside the United States, but in appropriate circumstances, the Secretary may, under paragraph (e) of this section, waive the applicability of some or all of the requirements of these regulations for research of this type.

(b) Research activities in which the only involvement of human subjects will be in one or more of the following categories are exempt from these regulations unless the research is covered by other subparts of this part.

(1) Research conducted in established or commonly accepted educational settings, involving normal educational practices, such as (i) research on regular and special education instructional strategies, or (ii) research on the effectiveness of or the comparison among instructional techniques, curricula, or classroom management methods.

(2) Research involving the use of educational tests (cognitive, diagnostic, aptitude, achievement), if information taken from these sources is recorded in such a manner that subjects cannot be identified, directly or through identifiers linked to the subjects.

(3) Research involving survey or interview procedures, except where all of the following conditions exist: (i) responses are recorded in such a manner that the human subjects can be identified directly or through identifiers linked to the subjects, (ii) the subject's responses, if they became known outside the research, could reasonably place the subject at risk of criminal or civil liability or be damaging to the subject's financial standing or employability, and (iii) the research deals with sensitive aspects of the subject's own behavior, such as illegal conduct, drug use, sexual behavior, or use of alcohol. All research involving survey or interview procedures is exempt, without exception, when the respondents are elected or appointed public officials or candidates for public office.

(4) Research involving the observation (including observation by participants) of public behavior, except where all of the following conditions exist: (i) observations are recorded in such a manner that the human subjects can be identified, directly or through identifiers linked to the subjects, (ii) the observations recorded about the individual, if they became known outside the research, could reasonably place the subject at the risk of criminal or civil liability or be damaging to the subject's financial standing or employability, and (iii) the research deals with sensitive aspects of the subject's own behavior such as illegal conduct, drug use, sexual behavior, or use of alcohol.

(5) Research involving the collection or study of existing data, documents, records, pathological specimens, or diagnostic specimens, if these sources are publicly available or if the information is recorded by the investigator in such a manner that subjects cannot be identified, directly or through identifiers linked to the subjects.

(6) Unless specifically required by statute (and except to the extent specified in paragraph (i), research and demonstration projects which are conducted by or subject to the approval of the Department of Health and Human Services, and which are designed to study, evaluate, or otherwise examine: (i) programs under the Social Security Act, or other public benefit or service programs; (ii) procedures for obtaining benefits or services under those programs; (iii) possible changes in or alternatives to those programs or procedures; or (iv) possible changes in methods or levels of payment for benefits or services under those program.

(c) The Secretary has final authority to determine whether a particular activity is covered by these regulations.

(d) The Secretary may require that specific research activities or classes of research activities conducted or funded by the Department, but not otherwise covered by these regulations, comply with some or all of these regulations.

(e) The Secretary may also waive applicability of these regulations to specific research activities or classes of research activities, otherwise covered by these regulations. Notices of these actions will be published in the *Federal Register* as they occur.

(f) No individual may receive Department funding for research covered by these regulations unless the individual is affiliated with or sponsored by an institution which assumes responsibility for the research under an assurance satisfying the requirements of this part, or the individual makes other arrangements with the Department.

(g) Compliance with these regulations will in no way render inapplicable pertinent federal, state, or local laws or regulations.

(h) Each subpart of these regulations contains a separate section describing to what the subpart applies. Research which is covered by more than one subpart shall comply with all applicable subparts.

(i) If, following review of proposed research activities that are exempt from these regulations under paragraph (b) (6), the Secretary determines that a research or demonstration project presents a danger to the physical, mental, or emotional well-being of a participant or subject of the research or demonstration project, then federal funds may not be expended for such a project without the written, informed consent of each participant or subject.

§ 46.102 Definitions.

(a) "Secretary" means the Secretary of Health and Human Services and any other officer or employee of the Department of Health and Human Services to whom authority has been delegated.

(b) "Department" or "HHS" means the Department of Health and Human Services.

(c) "Institution" means any public or private entity or agency (including federal, state, and other agencies).

(d) "Legally authorized representative" means an individual or judicial or other body authorized under applicable law to consent on behalf of perspective subject to the subject's participation in the procedure(s) involved in the research.

(e) "Research" means a systematic investigation designed to develop or contribute to generalizable knowledge. Activities which meet this definition constitute "research" for purposes of these regulations, whether or not they are supported or funded under a program which is considered research for other purposes. For example, some "demonstration" and "service" programs may include research activities.

(f) "Human subject" means a living individual about whom an investigator (whether professional or student) conducting research obtains (1) data through intervention or interaction with the individual, or (2) identifiable private information. "Intervention" includes both physical procedures by which data are gathered (for example, venipuncture) and manipulations of the subject or the subject's environment that are performed for research purposes. "Interaction" includes communication or interpersonal contact between investigator and subject. "Private information" includes information about behavior that occurs in a context in which an individual can reasonably expect that no observation or recording is taking place, and information which has been provided for specific purposes by an individual and which the individual can reasonably expect will not be made public (for example, a medical record). Private information must be individually identifiable (i.e., the identity of the subject is or may readily be ascertained by the investigator or associated with the information) in order for obtaining the information to constitute research involving human subjects.

(g) "Minimal risk" means that the risks of harm anticipated in the proposed research are not greater, considering probability and magnitude, than those ordinarily encountered in daily life or during the performance of routine physical or psychological examinations or tests.

(h) "Certification" means the official notification by the institution to the Department in accordance with the requirements of this part that a research project or activity involving human subjects has been reviewed and approved by the Institutional Review Board (IRB) in accordance with the approved assurance on file at HHS. (Certification is required when the research is funded by the Department and not otherwise exempt in accordance with § 46.101 (b)).

§ 46.111 Criteria for IRB approval of research.

(a) In order to approve research covered by these regulations the IRB shall determine that all of the following requirements are satisfied:

(1) Risks to subjects are minimized: (i) By using procedures which are consistent with sound research design and which do not unnecessarily expose subjects to risk, and (ii) whenever appropriate, by using procedures already being performed on the subjects for diagnostic or treatment purposes.

(2) Risks to subjects are reasonable in relation to anticipated benefits, if any, to subjects, and the importance of the knowledge that may reasonably be expected to result. In evaluating risks and benefits, the IRB should consider only those risks and benefits that may result from the research (as distinguished from risks and benefits of therapies subjects would receive even if not participating in the research). The IRB should not consider possible long-range effects of applying knowledge gained in the research (for example, the possible effects of the research on public policy) as among those research risks that fall within the purview of its responsibility.

(3) Selection of subjects is equitable. In making this assessment the IRB should take into account the purposes of the research and the setting in which the research will be conducted.

(4) Informed consent will be sought from each prospective subject or the subject's legally authorized representative, in accordance with, and to the extent required by § 46.116.

(5) Informed consent will be appropriately documented, in accordance with, and to the extent required by § 46.117.

(6) Where appropriate, the research plan makes adequate provision for monitoring the data collected to insure the safety of subjects.

(7) Where appropriate, there are adequate provisions to protect the privacy of subjects and to maintain the confidentiality of data.

(b) Where some or all of the subjects are likely to be vulnerable to coercion or undue influence, such as persons with acute or severe physical or mental illness, or persons who are economically or educationally disadvantaged, appropriate additional safeguards have been included in the study to protect the rights and welfare of these subjects.

§ 46.116 General requirements for informed consent.

Except as provided elsewhere in this or other subparts, no investigator may involve a human being as a subject in research covered by these regulations unless the investigator has obtained the legally effective informed consent of the subject or the subject's legally authorized representative. An investigator shall seek such consent only under circumstances that provide the prospective subject or the representative sufficient opportunity to consider whether or not to participate and that minimize the possibility of coercion or undue influence. The information that is given to the subject or the representative shall be in language understandable to the subject or the representative. No informed consent, whether oral or written, may include any exculpatory language through which the subject or the representative is made to waive or appear to waive any of the subject's legal rights, or release or appear to release the investigator, the sponsor, the institution or its agents from liability for negligence.

(a) Basic elements of informed consent. Except as provided in paragraph (c) or (d) of this section, in seeking informed consent the following information shall be provided to each subject:

(1) A statement that the study involves research, an explanation of the purposes of the research and the expected duration of the subject's participation, a description of the procedures to be followed, and identification of any procedures which are experimental;

(2) A description of any reasonably foreseeable risks or discomforts to the subject;

(3) A description of any benefits to the subject or to others which may reasonably be expected from the research;

(4) A disclosure of appropriate alternative procedures or courses of treatment, if any, that might be advantageous to the subject;

(5) A statement describing the extent, if any, to which confidentiality of records identifying the subject will be maintained;

(6) For research involving more than minimal risks, an explanation as to whether any compensation and an explanation as to whether any medical treatments are available if injury occurs and, if so, what they consist of, or where further information may be obtained;

(7) An explanation of whom to contact for answers to pertinent questions about the research and research subjects' rights, and whom to contact in the event of a research-related injury to the subject; and

(8) A statement that participation is voluntary, refusal to participate will involve no penalty or loss of benefits to which the subject is otherwise entitled, and the subject may discontinue participation at any time without penalty or loss of benefits to which the subject is otherwise entitled.

(b) Additional elements of informed consent. When appropriate, one or more of the following elements of information shall be provided to each subject:

(1) A statement that the particular treatment or procedure may involve risks to the subject (or to the embryo or fetus, if the subject is or may become pregnant) which are currently unforeseeable;

(2) Anticipated circumstances under which the subject's participation may be terminated by the investigator without regard to the subject's consent;

(3) Any additional costs to the subject that may result from participation in the research;

(4) The consequences of a subject's decision to withdraw from the research and procedures for orderly termination of participation by the subject;

(5) A statement that significant new findings developed during the course of the research which may relate to the subject's willingness to continue participation will be provided to the subject; and

(6) The approximate number of subjects involved in the study.

(c) An IRB may approve a consent procedure which does not include, or which alters, some or all of the elements of informed consent set forth above, or waive the requirement to obtain informed consent provided the IRB finds and documents that:

(1) The research or demonstration project is to be conducted by or subject to the approval of state or local government officials and is designed to study, evaluate, or otherwise examine: (i) programs under the Social Security Act, or other public benefit or service programs; (ii) procedures for obtaining benefits or services under these programs; (iii) possible changes in or alternatives to those programs or procedures; or (iv) possi-

ble changes in methods or levels of payment for benefits or services under those programs; and

(2) The research could not practicably be carried out without the waiver or alteration.

(d) An IRB may approve a consent procedure which does not include, or which alters, some or all of the elements of informed consent set forth above, or waive the requirements to obtain informed consent provided the IRB finds and documents that:

(1) The research involves no more than minimal risk to the subjects;

(2) The waiver or alteration will not adversely affect the rights and welfare of the subjects;

(3) The research could not practicably be carried out without the waiver or alternation; and

(4) Whenever appropriate, the subjects will be provided with additional pertinent information and participation.

(e) The informed consent requirements in these regulations are not intended to preempt any applicable federal, state, or local laws which require additional information to be disclosed in order for informed consent to be legally effective.

(f) Nothing in these regulations is intended to limit the authority of a physician to provide emergency medical care, to the extent the physician is permitted to do so under applicable federal, state, or local law.

§ 46.122 Use of federal funds.

Federal funds administered by the Department may not be expended for research involving human subjects unless the requirements of these regulations, including all subparts of these regulations, have been satisfied.

Subpart D—Additional Protections for Children Involved as Subjects in Research.

Source: 48 FR 9818, March 8, 1983

§ 46.401 To what do these regulations apply?

(a) This subpart applies to all research involving children as subjects, conducted or supported by the Department of Health and Human Services.

(1) This includes research conducted by Department employees, except that each head of an Operating Division of the Department may adopt

such nonsubstantive, procedural modifications as may be appropriate from an administrative standpoint.

(2) It also includes research conducted or supported by the Department of Health and Human Services outside the United States, but in appropriate circumstances, the Secretary may, under paragraph (e) of § 46.101 of Subpart A, waive the applicability of some or all of the requirements of these regulations for research of this type.

(b) Exemptions 91), (2), (5) and (6) as listed in Subpart A at § 46.101 (b) are applicable to this subpart. Exemption (4), research involving the observation of public behavior, listed as § 46.101 (b), is applicable to this subpart where the investigator(s) does not participate in the activities being observed. Exemption (3), research involving survey or interview procedures, listed at § 46.101 (b) does not apply to research covered by this subpart.

(c) The exceptions, additions, and provisions for waiver as they appear in paragraphs (c) through (i) of § 46.101 of Subpart A are applicable to this subpart.

§ 46.402 Definitions.

The definitions in § 46.102 of Subpart A shall be applicable to this subpart as well. In addition, as used in this subpart:

(a) "Children" are persons who have not attained the legal age for consent to treatments or procedures involved in the research, under the applicable law of the jurisdiction in which the research will be conducted.

(b) "Assent" means a child's affirmative agreement to participate in research. Mere failure to object should not, absent affirmative agreement, be construed as assent.

(c) "Permission" means the agreement of parent(s) or guardian to the participation of their child or ward in research.

(d) "Parent" means a child's biological or adoptive parent.

(e) "Guardian" means an individual who is authorized under applicable state or local law to consent on behalf of a child to general medical care.

§ 46.403 IRB duties.

In addition to other responsibilities assigned to IRBs under this part, each IRB shall review research covered by this subpart and approve only research which satisfies the conditions of all applicable sections of this subpart.

§ 46.404 Research not involving greater than minimal risk.

HHS will conduct or fund research in which the IRB finds that no greater than minimal risk to children is presented, only if the IRB finds that adequate provisions are made for soliciting the assent of the children and the permission of their parents or guardians, as set forth in § 46.408.

§ 46.405 Research involving greater than minimal risk but presenting the prospect of direct benefit to the individual subjects.

HHS will conduct or fund research in which the IRB finds that more than minimal risk to children is presented by an intervention or procedure that holds out the prospect of direct benefit for the individual subject, or by a monitoring procedure that is likely to contribute to the subject's well-being only if the IRB finds that:

(a) The risk is justified by the anticipated benefit to the subjects;

(b) The relations of the anticipated benefit to the risk is at least as favorable to the subjects as that presented by available alternative approaches; and

(c) Adequate provisions are made for soliciting the assent of the children and permission of their parents or guardians, as set forth in § 46.408.

§ 46.406 Research involving greater than minimal risk and no prospect of direct benefit to individual subjects, but likely to yield generalizable knowledge about the subject's disorder or condition.

HHS will conduct or fund research in which the IRB finds that more than minimal risk to children is presented by an intervention or procedure that does not hold out the prospect of direct benefit for the individual subject, or by a monitoring procedure which is not likely to contribute to the well-being of the subject, only if the IRB finds that:

(a) The risk represents a minor increase over minimal risk;

(b) The intervention or procedure presents experiences to subjects that are reasonably commensurate with those inherent in their actual or expected medical, dental, psychological, social, or educational situations;

(c) The intervention or procedure is likely to yield generalizable knowledge about the subjects' disorder or condition which is of vital importance for the understanding or amelioration of the subjects' disorder or condition; and

(d) Adequate provisions are made for soliciting assent of the children and permission of their parents or guardians, as set forth in § 46.408.

§ 46.407 Research not otherwise approvable which presents an opportunity to understand, prevent, or alleviate a serious problem affecting the health or welfare of children.

HHS will conduct or fund research that the IRB does not believe meets the requirements of §§ 46.404, 46.405, or 46.406 only if:

(a) The IRB finds that the research presents a reasonable opportunity to further the understanding, prevention, or alleviation of a serious problem affecting the health or welfare of children; and

(b) The Secretary, after consultation with a panel of experts in pertinent disciplines (for example: science, medicine, education, ethics, law) and following opportunity for public review and comment, has determined either: (1) That the research in fact satisfies the conditions of §§ 46.404, 46.405, or 46.406, as applicable, or (2) the following:

(i) The research presents a reasonable opportunity to further the understanding, prevention, or alleviation of a serious problem affecting the health or welfare of children;

(ii) The research will be conducted in accordance with sound ethical principles;

(iii) Adequate provisions are made for soliciting the assent of children and the permission of their parents or guardians, as set forth in § 46.408.

§ 46.408 Requirements for permission by parents or guardians and for assent by children.

(a) In addition to the determinations required under other applicable sections of this subpart, the IRB shall determine that adequate provisions are made for soliciting the assent of the children, when in the judgment of the IRB the children are capable of providing assent. In determining whether children are capable of assenting, the IRB shall take into account the ages, maturity, and psychological state of the children involved. This judgement may be made for all children to be involved in research under a particular protocol, or for each child, as the IRB deems appropriate. If the IRB determines that the capability of some or all of the children is so limited that they cannot reasonably be consulted or that the intervention or procedure involved in the research holds out a prospect of direct benefit that is important to the health or well-being of the children and is available only in the context of the research, the assent of the children is not a necessary condition for proceeding with the research. Even where the IRB determines that the subjects are capable of assenting, the IRB may still waive the assent requirement under circumstances in which consent may be waived in accord with § 46.116 of Subpart A.

(b) In addition to the determinations required under other applicable sections of this subpart, the IRB shall determine, in accordance with and to the extent that consent is required by § 46.116 of Subpart A, that adequate provisions are made for soliciting the permission of each child's parents or guardian. Where parental permission is to be obtained, the IRB may find that the permission of one parent is sufficient for research to be conducted under §§ 46.404 or 46.405. Where research is covered by §§ 46.406 or 46.407 and permission is to be obtained from parents, both parents must give their permission unless one parent is deceased, unknown, incompetent, or not reasonably available, or when only one parent has legal responsibility for the care and custody of the child.

(c) In addition to the provisions for waiver contained in § 46.116 of Subpart A, if the IRB determines that a research protocol is designed for conditions or for a subject population for which parental or guardian permission is not a reasonable requirement to protect the subjects (for example, neglected or abused children), it may waive the consent requirements in Subpart A of this part and paragraph (b) of this section, provided an appropriate mechanism for protecting the children who will participate as subjects in the research is substituted, and provided further that the waiver is not inconsistent with federal, state or local law. The choice of an appropriate mechanism would depend upon the nature and purpose of the activities described in the protocol, the risk and anticipated benefit to the research subjects, and their age, maturity, status, and condition.

(d) Permission by parents or guardians shall be documented in accordance with and to the extent required by § 46.117 of Subpart A.

(e) When the IRB determines that assent is required, it shall also determine whether and how assent must be documented.

§ 46.409 Wards.

(a) Children who are wards of the state or any other agency, institution, or entity can be included in research approved under §§ 46.406 or 46.407 only if such research is:

(1) Related to their status as wards; or

(2) Conducted in schools, camps, hospitals, institutions, or similar settings in which the majority of children involved as subjects are not wards.

(b) If the research is approved under paragraph (a) of this section, the IRB shall require appointment of an advocate for each child who is a ward, in addition to any other individual acting on behalf of the child as guardian or in loco parentis. One individual may serve as advocate for more than one child. The advocate shall be an individual who has the background and experience to act in, and agrees to act in, the best interests of the child for the duration of the child's participation in the research and who is not associated in any way (except in the role as advocate or member of the IRB) with the research, the investigator(s), or the guardian organization.

PART I

The Developmental Process

3

Developmental Changes in Research Risk and Benefit

A Changing Calculus of Concerns

ROSS A. THOMPSON

Behavioral scientists enlist children in their studies of social and psychological processes for a variety of reasons. Often they are concerned with normative changes in human development, such as the growth of emotional attachments; the emergence of empathy, guilt, or prosocial behavior; or the bases for achievement motivation. Sometimes they are interested in atypical developmental pathways, such as those observed in maltreated children or infants with congenital challenges. And increasingly, behavioral scientists are concerned with at-risk populations of children and youth, such as sexually active adolescents who are vulnerable to AIDS (see

AUTHOR'S NOTE: The issues discussed in this chapter have been developed by valuable and provocative conversations with numerous colleagues, especially colleagues on a Work Group on Ethical Issues in Social and Behavioral Research with Minors convened and sponsored by the Office for Protection from Research Risk of the National Institutes of Health, members of a faculty seminar on Ethics and the Professions at the University of Nebraska, and students and faculty in a Developmental Research Seminar also at the University of Nebraska. I am especially grateful for helpful comments on earlier drafts of this chapter from Robert Audi, Susan Crockenberg, Jan Jacobs, Robert Levine, Ruth Macklin, Gary Melton, Joan Sieber, and Barbara Stanley. This chapter is based on an earlier version of this discussion that appeared in *Child Development* in its February, 1990 issue.

chapter 8), or youth who are engaged in substance abuse or illegal behavior (see chapter 9).

Whatever their research purposes, behavioral scientists encounter formidable challenges in defining their ethical responsibilities to the children who participate in their research. Perhaps the most significant of these challenges is estimating risks and benefits to research participants. Because of their immaturity, young children are less capable of benefitting from the research experience and of defending their interests in research settings, and the risk-benefit assessment is additionally complicated because many of the harms children may encounter in behavioral research are psychological rather than physical in nature and are consequently more difficult to assess and predict. These considerations make the estimation of research risks and benefits in behavioral research a difficult task. Consider the following examples.

A 1-year-old infant and her mother are ushered into the research playroom by a smiling lab assistant. After a few minutes of instructions, the two are left alone for the beginning of a 21-minute procedure designed to appraise the security of their attachment relationship. During this period, a female stranger enters the room on two occasions to play with the baby. The mother also leaves the room on two occasions—once leaving the baby in the company of the stranger, and a second time leaving the child alone—during which the baby becomes markedly distressed. During their second reunion, the mother is disturbed to find that her child is not becoming soothed, but instead alternates clinging with pushing away and angry crying. The child is still fussing when the two leave the laboratory.

A 9-year-old boy enters the empty school classroom with the researcher who had been introduced to him just moments before. After a few minutes of getting acquainted, the researcher tells the boy that she is interested in his speed at completing jigsaw puzzles, and she gives him a puzzle to complete. He does so quickly and receives her admiration and praise in return. She then gives him four more puzzles, and for each one he is surprised to find that he is unable to finish it in the time provided. The researcher then asks him some questions about how he evaluates his abilities and efforts in completing puzzles, in finishing schoolwork, and in other areas of achievement. Before he leaves, she notes that the four puzzles were designed to be difficult to solve, so he should not feel badly about his performance. He then returns to his classroom, where he is in a special group for slow learners, wondering whether she told him the truth.

A 13-year-old girl enters the carpeted laboratory and is given a thick booklet of questionnaires involving vocabulary items, number problems, and other routine tests to complete. She is told by the researcher that he is preparing a subsequent part of the study for her in the next room, and under no circumstances should she enter that room until she is asked to do so. As she works on the problems, she notices some unusual sounds coming from the next room. Later, she watches another girl of the same age entering the room. Finally, compelled by her curiosity, she quickly opens the door to the room, notices that it is empty, and promptly returns to her work. When the researcher returns, he inquires about whether she looked into the next room, and she tells him that she did not. When she is told later that the researcher was interested in the conditions in which adolescents would violate an adult's request and that she had been observed throughout this episode from behind a one-way window, she feels mingled emotions of embarrassment and shame at disobeying the rule and subsequently lying about it, as well as anger at being deceived and resentment toward the researcher. Later that day, she begins wondering how honest a person she truly is and what her friends and parents would think if they knew how she behaved in the study.

In other procedures, preschoolers are observed in circumstances designed to elicit guilt (when they play with a doll that is designed to break) or shame (after drinking from a cup that leaks onto the child's shirt), or school-age children are interviewed after watching a movie about parental loss or nuclear warfare, or preadolescents' assessments of their peers are appraised systematically. In themselves, most research procedures include sufficient safeguards to ensure that harms to children are minimized, and the overwhelming majority of behavioral studies involving children are ethically unquestionable (Fisher & Brennan, in press). However, they crystallize the challenges inherent in estimating research risks to children in light of developmental changes in their vulnerability to the harms to which children are susceptible at various ages. They also illustrate the inherent difficulties in balancing risks against predicted benefits from research.

The purpose of this chapter is to outline a developmental perspective to research risks and benefits that will, I hope, assist researchers and institutional review boards (IRBs) in their efforts to articulate ethical responsibilities to children involved in behavioral research. In summary, I argue that a sensitive assessment of research risk involves acknowledging that risks vary with development in complex ways:

some decrease with the child's increasing age, whereas others increase as the child matures; and some risks fluctuate or remain essentially stable over development. As a consequence, it is necessary to consider different domains of research risk independently in estimating their potential effects on children of different ages, rather than assuming that, on the whole, vulnerability in research declines linearly with age. Moreover, the same is true of estimating the benefits of research participation that are enjoyed by the child: in most behavioral research, benefits change complexly with the child's age, and this change has important implications for the comparative evaluation of risks and benefits. Finally, any discussion of the assessment of risks and benefits in research must include consideration of *who* does the estimation, especially when the judging of the likelihood of risks and benefits is so probabilistic, and the final part of this chapter raises questions concerning the relative roles of researchers, parents, and children themselves in consenting to research participation.

Assessing Risks and Benefits in Behavioral Research With Children

The need to estimate sensitively the risks and benefits of research participation is well instituted in the ethical guidelines of behavioral researchers. Although the Ethical Principles of Psychologists of the American Psychological Association include no special provisions for research with children, psychologists are mandated not to use research procedures "likely to cause serious or lasting harm to a participant" unless the research "has great potential benefit" and informed and voluntary consent is obtained (American Psychological Association, 1990, p. 395). Likewise, the Ethical Standards for Research with Children of the Society for Research in Child Development mandate that researchers should use no procedure that "may harm the child either physically or psychologically," although defining this phrase is left to the investigator in consultation with colleagues. Researchers are encouraged also to weigh the "scientific and human value of the project" relative to the potential risks to which participants are exposed (Committee for Ethical Conduct in Child Development Research, 1990).

The National Commission for the Protection of Human Subjects of Biomedical and Behavioral Research (NCPHS) was created by Congress in 1974 to provide recommendations concerning the treatment of human participants in research, and in 1977 the commission issued a report entitled *Research Involving Children* (NCPHS, 1978). Based in part on the commission's recommendations, in 1983 the Department of Health and Human Services (DHHS) adopted agency regulations specifically pertaining to research involving children (DHHS, 1983). Various levels of research risk were established in these regulations. "Minimal risk" is defined as the risk of harm not greater than that "ordinarily encountered in daily life or during the performance of routine physical or psychological examinations or tests" (DHHS, 1983, 45 CFR 46.102[g]), and research studies involving no more than minimal risk can be supported by DHHS contingent on the permission of the child's parents or guardian(s) and the child's own assent. No requirement of predictable benefits either to the child, to the parents or guardian(s), or to society in general exists.

Research involving greater than minimal risk may be approved if it involves an intervention from which the child is likely to benefit directly, or a monitoring procedure that is likely to contribute to the child's "well-being," and an IRB finds that the risk can be justified by the benefits the child receives and the risk-benefit relation is no less favorable to the child than that from any available alternative procedure. These rather stringent criteria involving the relative balance of risks and benefits to the children who participate would appear to undermine the possibility that research involving greater than minimal risk could be approved if children do *not* benefit directly from the research experience. Such research, however, can be approved by an IRB contingent on a finding that the risk represents a "minor increase" over minimal risk, the procedure involves experiences that are commensurate with those involved in "actual or expected medical, dental, psychological, social, or educational situations," and the research is likely to yield "generalizable knowledge that is of "vital importance" for the understanding of the child's "disorder or condition" (DHHS, 1983, 45 CFR 46.406). The kinds of procedures that constitute a "minor increase" over minimal risk are not defined in these regulations, but the National Commission had recommended four guidelines: a common-sense estimation of risk, the researcher's prior experience with children in similar procedures, statistical data concerning the effects of these procedures, and the conditions of the research participants themselves. It is important, however, that the benefits against which these risks are weighed now include broader benefits to society in the form of generalizable knowledge.

Finally, research procedures that do not satisfy "minimal risk" or "minor increase" provisions may be approved nevertheless if the research "presents an opportunity to understand, prevent, or alleviate a serious problem affecting the health or welfare of children" (p. 16). This research requires additional review procedures and findings, however, not only by an IRB but also by the secretary of DHHS, as well as the opportunity for public review and comment. Although these DHHS regulations apply only to research that is funded or requires the approval of DHHS and its agencies, and major classes of research are exempt (such as research in educational settings concerning instructional techniques or classroom management methods; see Holder, 1988), these regulations have become the *de facto* guidelines applied by most IRBs in regulating behavioral research activity in most university settings.

Ethical Basis for Risk-Benefit Analysis

Because of the emphasis on justifying potentially harmful research procedures in terms of anticipated benefits to the child or to society, these professional and governmental guidelines seem to be based on an act-utilitarian approach to ethical analysis. But the ethical bases for this analysis are considerably more complex because these guidelines also impose certain immutable standards for research related to informed consent, confidentiality, and privacy, as well as the limits of acceptable risk. In fact, a combination of utilitarian and deontological viewpoints seems to shape these regulations (Macklin, 1982), and these viewpoints may be summarized in at least four broad ethical principles (NCPHS, 1979).

Research ethicists often begin from the first principle—a common principle of respect for persons, a chief aspect of which is autonomy. It finds expression in Kant's (1785/1959) categorical imperative of treating persons as ends in themselves, never solely as means to an end, but it can be justified also within a rule-utilitarian framework. In its broadest sense, the principle of respect for persons mandates the right of considerable individual self-determination in the research process, and respect for the wishes and decisions of research participants, as well as their values and beliefs. This principle is most fundamentally protected in procedures for obtaining informed consent, but it also underlies research regulations concerning individual privacy and the confidentiality of research materials, the freedom of participants to withdraw at any time, limits on deceptive research practices, and the importance of debriefing following research procedures.

The second principle underlying research ethics is the principle of nonmaleficence; that it is wrong to inflict harm on another, especially intentional or negligent harm. This principle requires researchers to minimize the risks of harm to research participants, however minor the risks may be.

When considered together with the third ethical principle of beneficence—the positive responsibility to remove existing harms and to provide benefits to others—the ethical basis for the risk-benefit analysis becomes apparent. On a broad level, researchers must be able to justify their study in terms of the potential benefits it promises, especially when research participation involves identifiable risks to participants. Researchers are thus commonly required to describe potential risks from research participation, to describe possible benefits from the research (to participants as well as to society), and to struggle with their calculus. Principles of nonmaleficence and beneficence function hand-in-hand in the ethical analysis of research; although the former is obligatory and the latter is supererogatory in ethical analysis, each is required to justify research procedures that involve meaningful and identifiable risks to participants.

Finally, the fourth ethical principle commonly used in the evaluation of research is justice: a fair distribution of goods, which entails the obligation to treat equally those who are equally situated, and to treat differently those who differ in relevant ways. The principle of justice fundamentally requires impartiality and fairness in the treatment of research participants. Distributive justice principles are influential in subject selection procedures, for example, especially in studies involving risk to participants or evaluating potentially beneficial treatments, therapies, or other interventions that may be denied to control or placebo group members. Justice also mandates efforts to ensure that research participants suffer no undesirable effects of their research involvement (which may be relevant to the design of dehoaxing and debriefing procedures), that they are treated equitably in light of their backgrounds and characteristics (which may affect the design of research procedures), and that unique vulnerabilities or resiliency of particular participants receive special consideration (sometimes in the context of additional procedures, conditions, treatments, or referral to others for special assistance).

The breadth of these ethical principles, together with the ambiguity of the regulatory language that instantiates them, means that they are unlikely to provide specific, clear applications to the thorny dilemmas researchers commonly face when designing a study. Their primary contribution, however, is in providing researchers and institutional regulators with a framework for thinking clearly and consistently in applying broad regulatory guidelines to specific research proposals. This contribution is important because the DHHS regulations provide little guidance concerning the meaning of such significant terms as "minimal risk," "minor increase over minimal risk," or the "vital importance" of "generalizable knowledge" concerning the "conditions" of research participants, and thus considerable interpretation of these terms is required. Maintaining thoughtful fidelity to such ethical principles makes this interpretive process less exclusively discretionary (by researchers and institutional regulators alike) and provides a foundation for useful discourse when the parties involved in research design and evaluation disagree over the ethical obligations of researchers.

Children as a Special Research Population

Within moral theory, children receive special consideration because of their unique characteristics. On the one hand, children cannot enjoy some of the moral prerogatives and responsibilities of mature individuals because of their more limited skills and capabilities, and this insufficiency is reflected (among other places) in court decisions recognizing that children are entitled to some—but not all—of the rights of privacy and self-determination granted to adults in our society (see chapter 4). On the other hand, children receive special benefits and protections to ensure that their needs and interests are safeguarded, and this consideration means that others (especially parents) are entrusted with significant responsibility for their protection and care. It is in this interesting combination of limited prerogatives and beneficent paternalism, both of which derive from a recognition of children's limitations, that the ethical analysis of research involving children includes special scrutiny. Careful thought is necessary because the characteristics of children introduce several unique vulnerabilities to their roles as research participants.

First, young children are likely to have greater difficulty than older children and adults in understanding the research process because of their more limited cognitive competencies and experiential background. Their capacity to make reasoned decisions concerning research participation, to understand the informed consent procedure and their freedom to withdraw, and to resist intrusions on their rights as research participants is limited. In a sense, young children have a very limited appreciation of the role of research participant, a conclusion that has important implications for the validity of some developmental research procedures, as well as for ethical analysis.

Second, young children are vulnerable also because of their limited social power. Parents and other adults exercise proxy consent for children, and children's institutionalization in extrafamilial care centers, schools, and other settings further reduces their power to exercise independent decision making concerning their research participation, or to resist intrusions on their rights as research participants. Although children's assent is encouraged by existing regulations, for example, it may be difficult for children to dissent from research participation because their invitation to participate typically occurs in a context of prior parental permission, institutional support, and adults' interests in furthering the research enterprise. For the same reasons, young children's social power to resist distressing, demeaning, coercive, or psychologically invasive research procedures also may be quite limited. Consequently, children may not only experience pressure to participate, but also to act and respond in the research setting in ways that are inconsistent with the child's own wishes or desires, violative of the child's beliefs, or otherwise self-defeating.

Third, young children are vulnerable as research participants because of their ambiguous legal status as minors that both protects and limits their rights (Baumrind, 1978; Melton, 1987). Because of this status, parents make fundamental decisions not only concerning the research participation of offspring (with parents exercising proxy consent), but also concerning the disposition of research materials, the uses of many direct benefits from research participation, children's withdrawal from research, and many other prerogatives that are normally made by the research participant alone. Although parents do so in the interests of offspring, it is unwise to assume that parental and child interests are always identical in these situations, and parental decision making may be motivated by self-interested considerations as well. Professional and institutional regulations, however, do not clearly indicate how disagreements between parent and offspring concerning research prerogatives should be resolved, and DHHS regulations include a number of provisions for waiving child assent requirements when parents consent to their research participation (see also Koocher & Keith-Spiegel, 1990; Pence, 1980). Consequently, children have uniquely little control over many fundamental aspects of research participation that are guaranteed for other participants.

For these reasons, the ethical analysis of research commonly begins with the assumption that children are particularly vulnerable research participants and that studies involving children require special scrutiny to ensure that their rights and needs are protected. Moreover, it is assumed commonly that the younger the children who participate, the more vulnerable they are in research because of the enhanced limitations in cognition and reasoning, experience, social power, and other features that limit their capacity to protect their rights as research participants. Consequently, research protocols involving younger populations typically receive stricter scrutiny. Within this essentially linear portrayal of developmental changes in vulnerability to research risk, researchers and institutional regulators commonly assume that with increasing age—and corollary increases in cognitive competencies, experiential background, and other changing capabilities—vulnerability declines and safeguards against harms in research need not be so stringent. Researchers consequently are encouraged to think more carefully and conservatively when designing research procedures for younger populations.

This developmental portrayal of changes in vulnerability to research risk can sensitize researchers and institutional regulators to the fact that "children" constitute a very heterogeneous research population, varying significantly in their capabilities and characteristics that have important implications for the ethical obligations of researchers. Research procedures that would be extremely stressful for an infant may have a negligible effect on an adolescent, for example. It is not, however, the only developmental portrayal that might be useful in the ethical review of research. Consider, for example, the kind of developmental model implicitly incorporated into current DHHS regulations outlined above. By defining "minimal risk" in terms of the risk of harms the child ordinarily encounters in daily life, these regulations suggest that as a child's normative life experiences change with increasing age—in accord with the child's growing competencies and experiential background—the norms governing acceptable levels of research risk must be revised comparably to encompass these changing experiences. By this standard, therefore, research procedures that would ordinarily not be permitted at an early age (e.g., extended separations from parents) might be permissible at a later age. On the other hand, procedures that would be allowed with young children because they are part of children's ordinary life experiences (e.g., violations of personal space and close physical contact with unfamiliar adults) might not be permitted in later years, when these experiences are not as typical.

The value of the developmental model incorporated within DHHS regulations is that it alerts us to the fact that different domains of research risk must be evaluated independently because they vary differently with the age of the child. Some risks increase with the child's increasing age; others are likely to decrease. Potential harms to which very young children are especially vulnerable (owing, for example, to their emotional dependence on caregivers) are not significant concerns with older children, whereas older children may be uniquely vulnerable to certain risks (such as threats to the self-concept) that are unlikely to occur with infants or very young children. Consequently, it is necessary to examine different domains of research risk independently to examine developmental changes in their potential effects on children. Defining risk in terms of age-related changes in normative life experience is one way of doing so.

The major shortcoming to the DHHS developmental model is that it potentially can be used to justify research procedures that, for other reasons, one might regard as ethically questionable. Children who live in dangerous neighborhoods or have been maltreated or are substance abusers experience dangerous and risky everyday life conditions that cannot justify the incorporation of such risks into research procedures, because doing so would violate ethical principles of respect for persons and nonmaleficence. Even if we assume that the DHHS regulations for "minimal risk" should be interpreted to refer only to the risks normally encountered by children growing up in safe, caring environments (cf. Koocher & Keith-Spiegel, 1990; chapter 5, this volume), problems remain in applying this formulation. For example, young children regularly experience invasions of their bodily and personal privacy by parents, teachers, and other adults, but it is not necessarily true that this justifies similar privacy invasions in the research context (see chapter 4). Older children and adolescents commonly encounter experiences at school and with peers that threaten their self-image, including unfavorable academic performance evaluations, teasing concerning personal or physical characteristics, and spontaneous, as well as elicited, social comparison. It is not clear that these normative life experiences provide a justification for considering comparable experiences in a research context to be "minimal risk," because of the ethical dilemmas they present when these experiences are inflicted for research purposes. In short, the DHHS developmental formulation sensitizes us to the importance of considering different domains of research risk independently for their changing developmental consequences, but it fails to define minimal standards of fair or decent treatment of children as research participants. By defining what is "minimal risk" in terms of what is normative in the child's life experience, it potentially justifies researchers acting in ways that undermine the child even though these experiences may be familiar to the child.

A New Developmental Formulation

These conclusions suggest that though children merit special consideration as research participants, the nature of this consideration is difficult to define precisely. Although children as a class of research participants deserve special concern because of their unique vulnerabilities vis-à-vis adults, "children" embraces a remarkably heterogeneous group of individuals who vary significantly in their developmental capabilities. Consequently, any assessment of vulnerability to research risk must include consideration of how changing cognitive skills, experiential background, and social power modifies the constellation of vulnerabilities that children experience at each age. It is apparent that simple, straightforward linear development portrayals—such as the view that children generally become less vulnerable to research risk with increasing age—are inadequate because, although children become less vulnerable to certain domains of research risk as they mature, they become more vulnerable to other domains with increasing age. In a sense, the same cognitive and experiential limitations that make younger children more susceptible to certain harms also buffer them against others to which older children are more vulnerable. Moreover, any comprehensive developmental portrayal of research vulnerability must help also to define minimal standards of fair and decent treatment of children who are research participants.

Unfortunately, a more adequate developmental portrayal of research vulnerability is necessarily a more complex one. It requires considering independently different domains of research risk and outlining age-related changes in children's vulnerability that may be linear, curvilinear, or essentially stable over developmental time. Vulnerability to research risks changes complexly with development because psychological development is a complex phenomenon. Such a portrayal must draw upon existing research knowledge concerning children's cognitive, socioemotional, and personality development, and thus is refined continuously as new research yields new insights into these developmental processes.

As a catalyst to the generation of such a comprehensive developmental model, I offer in this section some general guidelines related to vulnerability in research that appear to be well supported by the existing research literature. This discussion draws upon an incisive analysis by Maccoby (1983) to provide examples of how susceptibility to different research risks varies with the child's development (see Thompson, 1990c, for further details). These guidelines (in some cases, working hypotheses) may be framed in terms of broad propositions.

1. *In general, the younger the child the greater the possibility of general behavioral and socioemotional disorganization accompanying stressful experiences. With increasing age, the child's growing repertoire of coping skills permits greater adaptive functioning in the face of stress.* The research literature on the development of emotional self-regulation and coping (e.g., Kopp, 1989; Meerum Terwogt & Olthof, 1989; Thompson, 1990b) indicates that young children rely on external supports for coping with stressful circumstances (e.g., the assistance of caregivers and other adults, reliance on security objects, etc.), but that with increasing age children acquire a broadening repertoire of emotional self-regulatory strategies that can be applied flexibly to different situations. While the young infant cries inconsolably until a nurturant adult intervenes, the toddler can use a rudimentary repertoire of self-soothing behaviors, the preschooler can reflect on and talk about her or his feelings, the grade-school child can directly alter emotional arousal through distracting mental imagery or self-coaching, and the adolescent has sufficient awareness of her or his own idiosyncratic emotional style to institute strategies that are personally well suited to regulating emotional experience. As a consequence, infants and young children are at greater risk for being

overwhelmed by stressful research procedures at the moment they occur. Their reliance on the assistance of caregivers and the availability of a familiar setting and objects suggests that young children's coping skills are fostered by the presence of these features in a research setting. Thus, stressful research procedures that occur at home or in a familiar care setting with a caregiver present not only benefit from ecological validity but also foster the young child's coping with the demands of the research.

2. *Threats to a child's self-concept become more stressful with increasing age as children develop a more comprehensive, coherent, and integrated self-image, become more invested in an enduring identity, and acquire a more sophisticated understanding of the components of the self by which the self-concept becomes progressively modified and reshaped.* The content, organization, and structure of self-understanding change markedly from infancy through adolescence (Damon & Hart, 1982; Harter, 1983). Whereas preschoolers are concrete, physicalistic, and material in how they describe themselves, older school-age children and adolescents exhibit more abstract, psychological, and integrated systems of self-understanding. Moreover, various elements of a child's self-referent beliefs (such as the understanding of one's various skills and limitations) become progressively more differentiated and hierarchically integrated with increasing age. Whereas the preschooler tends to provide self-evaluative judgments in discrete situations without integrating these judgments into a comprehensive self-concept, the older grade-school child attempts to find consistency among diverse attributes to the self, and the adolescent begins to organize these self-referent beliefs into a broader, coherent system of self-understanding (i.e., an identity). Finally, children acquire a greater capacity for self-criticism as they acquire a better understanding of the determinants of individual differences in ability and effort (Nicholls, 1978). Consequently, whereas preschoolers are likely to remain optimistic in the face of performance failure, older grade-school children are more susceptible to learned helplessness and diminished self-esteem (Dweck & Elliot, 1983; Fincham & Cain, 1986).

These conclusions have important implications for developmental changes in vulnerability to research risk because they suggest that research experiences that threaten the child's self-concept (such as induced failure or deceptive performance evaluations or genuinely poor performance in tests of achievement, altruism, sociability, or other socially valued characteristics) are likely to be more stressful for older children than for younger children, because they are more likely to be internalized, provoke worried self-reflection, and threaten broader aspects of self-esteem. Moreover, because the self-concept becomes more refined with increasing age—that is, it reflects a more realistic appraisal of the child's genuine strengths and weaknesses versus the optimistic and unrealistic self-confidence of younger children—threats to the self-concept in research are likely to have a greater impact on older children because they contribute to the child's own self-criticism.

A developmental period of especially heightened vulnerability to these influences may exist in middle childhood when the child's self-referent beliefs are maturing but during which self-perceptions remain relatively flexible and can be influenced by the short-term performance evaluations that occur during research. By adolescence, vulnerability to these risks probably declines because children have developed a more consolidated and coherent system of self-referent beliefs that are less affected by situationally specific evaluative feedback of the kind encountered in most research situations. Adolescents, in other words, are more likely to doubt the feedback they receive than to doubt themselves when they learn they have performed poorly in research, because their self-understanding is more sophisticated, consolidated, and secure than in middle childhood. Thus, the developmental changes in vulnerability described here are curvilinear rather than linear, with middle childhood a period of heightened vulnerability to threats to the self-concept resulting from research experiences.

3. *Social comparison information becomes a more significant mode of self-evaluation with increasing age.* It is not until middle childhood that children spontaneously tend to incorporate a comparative metric into their self-evaluations: they increasingly judge their performance by the standards of others' performances (Dweck & Elliott, 1983; Ruble, 1983). As a consequence, older children may be more vulnerable to explicit or implied comparisons of their research performance with others and apt to incorporate this information into their own evaluations of their abilities; this developmental trend probably extends through adolescence. Moreover, older children may also be more sensitive to the evaluations of others to whom their research performance is disseminated, such as to parents or teachers. Thus, the feedback children receive about their performance in research settings

is likely to have a much different impact, depending on the children's age and self-evaluative skills and their concerns that this feedback will be transmitted to others whose esteem they value.

4. *The capacity to make sophisticated psychological inferences of others' motives, attitudes, and feelings increases with age. This domain of psychological inferences includes inferences about others' reactions to oneself.* The ability to infer sensitively another's feelings or motives is an accomplishment of the late preschool years, but it may not be until middle childhood that youngsters become proficient at inferring another's feelings and attitudes *toward oneself* because this requires divorcing one's self-perceptions from the perceptions of oneself by other people (Shantz, 1983). As a consequence, while younger children may be oblivious to the subtle cues, demands, and judgments of their performance that occur during research, older grade-school children will discern more sensitively these implicit messages and may be adversely influenced as a result of feeling compelled to divulge confidential information or to question the legitimacy of their judgments or in other ways experience subtle but significant coercion to respond in uncomfortable or inappropriate ways. This developmental change in sensitivity to others' attitudes and judgments has implications not only for the ethics of research procedures but also for the validity of research findings when children are influenced to act in an ungenuine manner.

It is worth noting, however, that this developmental change is a double-edged sword: it may contribute also to the enhanced capacity of older children to defend their interests as research participants. Once children have acquired an awareness that others may have attitudes and motives that are not overtly apparent but must instead be inferred from subtle cues, they are likely to approach research settings with greater skepticism concerning the researcher's true intentions and motives. In other words, whereas younger children are prone to accept research tasks at face value, older children are more likely to question research instructions, especially those that might appear to be deceptive or manipulative. Their greater skeptism, however, also has benefits and risks for older children. Although it enables them to approach research tasks with greater skepticism and awareness—with the consequent capacity to resist significant intrusions on their rights to be fully and accurately informed about the nature of these tasks this skepticism also may be a source of added stress and uncertainty. Whereas younger children are likely to believe the researcher's portrayal of research tasks as "a game," for example, other children are not only more likely to be disbelieving but are likely to associate conceptually the research experience with other authority-oriented evaluative experiences. The fifth-grader who asks the researcher "What are you *really* after?" may be doing so both to defend against being deceived, but also because of the anxiety that uncertainty naturally evokes.

5. *Once such self-conscious emotional reactions as shame, guilt, embarrassment, and pride are acquired initially, young children may be more vulnerable to their arousal because of their limited understanding of these emotions.* Self-conscious emotions emerge later developmentally than do the primary emotions (e.g., fear, anger, happiness, and sadness) because they rely on requisites of self-understanding and self-awareness (Campos, Barrett, Lamb, Goldsmith, & Stenberg, 1983). But with their emergence in the preschool years, evidence exists that young children overextend the meanings of such emotions as guilt and embarrassment to apply to a broader range of circumstances than those for which they are appropriate. For example, preschoolers and young school-age children report feeling guilty in situations for which they are not personally responsible, perhaps because of exaggerated perceptions of their own agency or confusion concerning intentionality (Graham, Doubleday, & Guarino, 1984; Harter, 1983; Thompson, 1987). It is not until children are 7 to 8 years old that they better understand that guilt is more appropriate only to situations in which they are personally culpable for negative situations. A similar developmental course may be true also of such other negative self-conscious emotions as shame.

These considerations suggest that once these self-conscious emotions have emerged developmentally, young children may be especially vulnerable to their arousal in inappropriate or unexpected circumstances because of their more limited understanding of the bases for these emotional experiences; this may be true especially in research contexts evaluating children's reactions to competition or to feedback concerning their performance or in which they experience negative situations for which their responsibility may be unclear. With more refined understanding during the grade-school years, vulnerability to these emotions may decline somewhat as children better understand the causal circumstances with which these emotions are associated. There may be, however, another developmental resurgence of susceptibility to self-conscious emotional reactions during adolescence, when some unique features of adolescent cognition combine with the demands of the peer environment to heighten susceptibility to such emotions as embarrassment, shame, and guilt (albeit for different reasons from the earlier period of developmental vulnerability; Coleman, 1980; Elkind, 1967). Thus, I am describing a rather complex curvilinear trend: very young children are buffered against these emotions because of their nascent emotional understanding, following by a period of heightened vulnerability during the preschool years due to their incomplete understanding of these emotions, and then diminished vulnerability during the grade-school years as children master the causal antecedents of these emotions, followed by another period of increased susceptibility owing to features of reasoning and peer relations in adolescence and its probable gradual decline during young adulthood.

6. *Young children's understanding of authority renders them more vulnerable to coercive manipulations than older children, for whom authority relations are better balanced by an understanding of individual rights. Furthermore, young children's trust of authorities makes them more vulnerable to being deceived in research.* While children in the preschool and early grade-school years tend to regard unfamiliar authorities as legitimate and powerful individuals who mandate obedience because of their intrinsically superior qualities, older children legitimate authorities by virtue of their training or experience and obey them because of respect for authority rather than unilateral reverence (Damon, 1977; Piaget, 1932/1965; Shantz, 1983). Authority relations increasingly become viewed as a cooperative, consensual compact adopted for the welfare of all. In research settings, therefore, younger children are more likely to respond to researchers with immediate compliance even when they encounter unreasonable or illegitimate demands, and they are more susceptible to deceptive or coercive research practices as a result. By contrast, older children are more likely to question spontaneously a researcher's requests, and their perceptions of the adult's legitimacy may be undermined by demands that they perceive as unreasonable. Regarding their research participation as their cooperative contribution to the researcher's efforts, the more mature understanding of authority relations by older children (as well as their capacity to speculate concerning another's intentions and motives) heightens the likelihood that they will discontinue research participation when they encounter demands that they consider unreasonable and that they will defend better their interests as research participants in other ways as well.

7. *Privacy interests and concerns increase and become more differ-entiated as children mature, and broaden from an initial focus on physical and possessional privacy to include concerns with informa-tional privacy.* With increasing age, personal privacy becomes an im-portant marker of independence and self-esteem, but children's privacy concerns change with growth in self-understanding. Children initially exhibit greater concern with establishing a physical location of their own (i.e., territorial privacy, such as a bedroom) and the in-tegrity of personal possessions (i.e., possessional privacy), but at later ages this concern extends to the control of others' knowledge of one's associations, activities, and interests (i.e., informational privacy; see chapter 4; Melton, 1983; Wolfe, 1978). This change suggests that children become increasingly vulnerable to perceived privacy intru-sions in research settings with increasing age, with older children and adolescents more likely than younger children to experience certain inquiries or requests as unduly intrusive or threatening. Moreover, to the extent that researchers gain access to personal information about research participants without their consent (e.g., data from school re-cords via parental permission), older children are especially likely to view this access as a breach of informational privacy. The same may be true of feedback concerning children's research performance that is routinely returned to parents and school administrators.

8. *With increasing age, children are likely to become more sensi-tive to cultural and socioeconomic biases in research that reflect neg-atively on the child's background, family, or previous experiences.* With developmental changes in the breadth and coherence of the self-concept, children are likely to identify themselves increasingly as members of broader social groups, including racial, ethnic, and socio-economic groups. As a consequence, their vulnerability and sensitiv-ity to overt and subtle biases in the research process is likely to increase with age.

These propositions do not, of course, exhaust the range of develop-mental changes in skills and capabilities that have important implica-tions for children's vulnerability to research risk. They illustrate the complexity of estimating how children of different ages will be influ-enced by research procedures. For some domains of risk, children become less vulnerable as they mature; for other domains, vulnera-bility escalates with increasing age; for other areas, developmen-tal changes are curvilinear or minimal. Consequently, a somewhat different set of considerations may be preeminent in the ethical review of research with children of one age compared with another.

In longitudinal research this changing calculus of concerns has especially important implications because it indicates that new domains of vulnerability are likely to emerge for consideration as the research cohort ages. Even though a longitudinal study was approved thoughtfully by an IRB at the initiation of the research, periodic reevaluations may be needed to ensure that the changing matrix of research risks are addressed appropriately as children mature. Potential harms that were irrelevant when the children were young may assume importance if similar procedures are used when children are older.

Taken together, these considerations indicate that a substantially more complex but sensitive analysis of developmental changes in vulnerability to research risk is needed to guide ethical decision making in behavioral research involving minors. Complexity is enhanced, however, not only because of the influence of developmental changes in children's skills and capabilities, but also because of individual differences between children at any age that may have implications also for their vulnerability to research risk. I now turn to a consideration of individual differences in children's backgrounds and characteristics.

Individual Differences in Vulnerability and Resiliency

Just as the term *children* embraces a very heterogeneous developmental population, so also the term encompasses a diverse range of backgrounds, characteristics, and prior experiences for children of any particular age. In many instances the special characteristics of the children who participate mandate special consideration in the ethical review of research, either because these characteristics introduce special vulnerabilities or provide added resiliency to research risks.

Consider, for example, the characteristics of maltreated children, who are frequently the focus of developmental investigations. Many elements of risk assessment must be calibrated somewhat differently for this special population. For example, because maltreating parents may not be reliable advocates for the interests of their offspring and may be especially concerned with detection of abusive behavior, issues of proxy consent must be reconsidered in studies using maltreated populations or samples at high risk for parental abuse. Supplementary consent procedures may be necessary.

Maltreated children also share other characteristics that are likely to make them somewhat more vulnerable to certain domains of research risk (Aber & Cicchetti, 1984; Cicchetti, 1990). They exhibit an acute sensitivity to aggressive stimuli and may be more prone to perceive ambiguous situations as threatening; they have diminished self-esteem and impaired perceptions of personal competence; and they respond atypically to novel adults, sometimes showing aloof disinterest and at other times exhibiting clingy dependency. As a consequence, maltreated children may be at greater risk in procedures that are stressful, threaten self-esteem, require focused interaction with a stranger, require evaluations of their competence, or involve experiences that are ambiguous and could be interpreted potentially as aggressive and threatening. In addition, just as the consequences of maltreatment change with age, so also the research vulnerabilities of maltreated children vary with their developmental status (Aber & Cicchetti, 1984). As a consequence, estimating the domains of research risk to which this special population of children are especially vulnerable requires considerable sensitivity and careful thought.

Other populations of children mandate similar consideration. When at-risk populations of children are identified for study (such as adolescent substance abusers, children who have suffered traumatic experiences, or the offspring of adults with emotional disturbances), researchers must be careful that the perceptions of these children by custodians from whom permission is sought are not biased by the description of the selection criteria that labels children in disadvantageous ways. With such populations, parental expectations concerning potential benefits the child may receive from research participation should be monitored also, because parents of at-risk children may regard *any* contact with professionals as a means of assisting the child, and this regard may influence proxy consent (Fisher & Rosendahl, in press). Children's own assent to research participation may be influenced by their inferences concerning the researcher's connections with the authority relations or service systems that directly affect the child, and consequently the delineation of the researcher's role vis-à-vis other adults in the child's experience (e.g., school personnel, counselors, medical staff, day-care workers, etc.) should be defined clearly. In Grisso's (1981) study of incarcerated juveniles, for example, most youth believed (despite disclaimers) that researchers were part of the juvenile justice system, and many were concerned that if they did not agree to participate they would be punished for doing so by the court. Similar concerns are likely to attend the decisions of children whose research participation is solicited in the context of the medical, counseling, or academic services they receive.

Thus, the backgrounds, prior experiences, and other characteristics of children sometimes introduce special vulnerabilities to the role of research participant. On other occasions, however, these characteristics may equip them with greater resiliency and enhance their capacities to make meaningful decisions concerning research participation and to defend their interests in research settings. In a general sense the law has long recognized this possibility in the special prerogatives accorded those deemed "emancipated minors" or "mature minors" who can engage in independent decision making that other adolescents may be denied. Although the criteria for identifying a "mature minor" are vague (see, for example, *Belotti v. Baird* [1979]), this status is defined in part by the capacity to make informed decisions independently of parents, and this is why the designation of "mature minor" is relevant to efforts to waive parental consent requirements in research by substituting the child's own assent (see chapter 6). Thus, the backgrounds and other characteristics of children may be not only vulnerability enhancing, but may introduce on other occasions greater resiliency in children's involvement in research.

Determining whether vulnerability or resiliency is enhanced for a particular research population can be a challenging enterprise and requires a detailed task-analysis of the various demands involved in the research procedure, as well as a broad understanding of the pertinent characteristics of the population of children under study. When making a determination of whether a child is capable of giving independent consent to research participation, an individualized assessment of the child's understanding of the research and his or her role in it may also be necessary (see chapter 6).

Taken together, it appears that a developmental analysis of vulnerability to research risk is complicated additionally by the necessity of considering seriously the special characteristics of the population under study and whether these characteristics introduce greater vulnerability or enhanced resiliency to research procedures. This necessity means that doing a careful ethical analysis of research risk in studies involving children is a difficult, demanding challenge.

Estimating Benefits

As earlier noted, professional and federal regulations governing research with children require estimations not only of the risks that children may encounter but also of benefits from the research. There are, of course, many potential benefits that can be derived from social and behavioral research findings. On the most general level, knowledge of human conditions is deepened and can have current and future benefits for society. In more specific terms, research findings may address particular social needs; advance knowledge identifying helpful interventions in therapy, education, or public policy-making; and usefully shape public perceptions of human functioning as findings are disseminated in the popular media. As the result of decades of research on infant-mother attachment relations, for example, a body of knowledge currently exists that has valuable applications to issues of child custody, child maltreatment, adoption and foster care, infant day care, and early mental health concerns (Thompson, 1988, 1990a; Thompson & Jacobs, in press). Basic research on parenting, language development, emotional growth, and a variety of other developmental issues similarly has found important social applications.

Children may benefit directly from their research participation. Research activities are typically pleasant, sometimes interesting, and children often learn from their experiences in research and receive affirming responses from the researcher. Some have argued that children's moral education is advanced also through research participation as children give altruistically of their time and efforts for the benefit of the researcher or society (Bartholome, 1976). Thus, children may enjoy certain direct benefits from their research participation that supplement the broader social benefits that research findings sometimes provide.

Many of these direct benefits vary with the age of the child, however, and thus a sensitive risk-benefit assessment incorporates an analysis of how benefits—like risks—vary with development. Although children at most ages can enjoy the benefits provided by pleasant research experiences, for example, their capacity to appreciate how research participation advances human knowledge depends on their understanding of the nature of research, their contributions as a research participant, and the scientific process. Few children before middle childhood are likely to grasp these complexities, and thus the moral education provided by research participation is unlikely to be a significant benefit of research participation before this time. In general, information that is provided a child during debriefing constitutes a research benefit only insofar as it is appropriate to the child's level of understanding, and debriefing is generally likely to be of very limited value for young children because of the complexity of the questions underlying most developmental research and the procedures designed to answer those questions. On the other hand, younger children may enjoy especially the straightforward pleasures of completing research tasks and receiving in return the praise of the researcher in a manner that older children and adolescents do not, and these facets of the research experience may be some of their direct benefits from research participation. Thus, many potential direct benefits of research participation are, like risks, developmentally calibrated in complex ways.

Estimating research risks and benefits in light of a child's developmental capabilities is a special challenge when considering the effects of dehoaxing procedures, which are intended to ameliorate the consequences of false information provided the child earlier in the research. When children are told, for example, that they have performed poorly on tasks when this was untrue, or they are provided deceptive instructions for the research, dehoaxing is intended to reduce or eliminate the negative consequences of this false information. For several reasons it is likely that dehoaxing procedures are ineffective with young children and thus constitute neither a research benefit nor undermine the risks of deceptive or misleading information. First, understanding deception tactics during dehoaxing requires recursive reasoning (e.g., "I know that you would think this way when I did this . . .") that is conceptually very demanding for preschool and young grade-school children to understand. Second, deception tactics are also complex and may be especially difficult for young children to understand when debriefing requires dehoaxing a set of earlier, convincing instructions from the researcher that children had trusted to be true. Finally, because young children often have difficulty reevaluating past performance in light of a subsequent standard, they may not spontaneously reappraise their earlier performance evaluations in light of what they are told subsequently about the nature of the task or the feedback they had received previously. For these reasons, when deceptive or false feedback procedures are included in research involving young children, alternative approaches are probably necessary to reduce the harms inherent in these procedures. These approaches might include additional trials in which children succeed at tasks on which they had failed previously, or opportunities to reverse the roles of researcher and subject when deceptive instructions are used.

Taken together, developmental considerations pertaining to research benefits are important for at least two reasons. First, they sensitize us to the fact that the direct benefits enjoyed by children as research participants are at least as important as the broader societal gains provided by research findings. Indeed, as I shall suggest below, ethical principles of justice make them preeminent, especially when participants experience meaningful research risks. Second, in the comparative evaluation of research risks and benefits, incrementing the benefits directly enjoyed by research participants is one means of creating a more favorable balance between the two. Heightening benefits to the children who participate in research is seldom considered carefully by behavioral researchers, and a developmental analysis of research benefits provides one means of thoughtfully and sensitively considering how this might be accomplished.

Risks and Benefits Compared

This developmental analysis of children's vulnerability to research risk has focused on risks to children's self-esteem, coping with stress, threats of embarrassment, privacy violations, pressures to cooperate with uncomfortable research procedures, and other psychological harms that may be encountered in behavioral research. At least two features of these harms distinguish them from the risks of physical harm, disability, or infection that may be encountered in biomedical studies or other classes of research. First, these harms seem rather benign by comparison and usually do not receive special scrutiny either by researchers or by institutional regulators. Indeed, the preceding analysis has a highly risk-aversive quality if it is read as an argument for stricter scrutiny of developmental research protocols under the federal standards of "minimal risk." Its purpose, however, is to heighten the sensitivity of the research community, as well as institutional regulators, to dimensions of psychological harm encountered in research that do not usually exceed "minimal risk" standards but merit attention anyway. Insofar as researchers are mandated ethically to minimize potential harms to research participants regardless of their severity, this analysis may be a useful contribution to this goal.

Second, because these potential harms are psychological in nature, developmental changes in risk are significantly more complicated than the physical risks of biomedical research and, as I have argued, may increase, decrease, or change in more complex fashion with developmental time. This complexity makes their prediction and assessment significantly more complicated as well, such that estimating the potential risks to research participants is, in many ways, an indeterminate task. In the end, because estimations of research risk require an acute consideration of developmental changes, as well as individual characteristics, the estimation is at least highly complex and probabilistic. The same is arguably true in the estimation of potential benefits from the research, whether experienced directly by research participants or by society at large.

This uncertainty has important implications for the comparative evaluation of research risks and benefits that is mandated both by professional research guidelines and by federal regulations concerning research with children. In these guidelines, researchers and institutional regulators are mandated to weigh the comparatively predicted risks and potential benefits of the research, approaching the ethical review process as a threshold concern: can the level of risk to children be justified by the anticipated benefits of research results? Once a researcher and an IRB can answer affirmatively, institutional requirements of ethical review are satisfied. But how easy is it ethically to weigh risks and benefits when each is hard to estimate? In behavioral research psychological risks are more paramount; this comparative evaluation requires making probabilistic judgments with widely varying degrees of certainty.

For other reasons, as well, the risk-benefit comparison is a problematic basis for the ethical review of research. In most behavioral research, those who assume the risks of research participation do not enjoy the benefits of research findings (especially if they are young children), and thus the comparison of risks and benefits involves the relative evaluation of things that are *not* comparable. In other words, risks are proximal to the children who participate, while benefits are distal. Principles of justice mandate that a risk-benefit calculus should be calibrated according to who are the bearers of risk and who enjoy the benefits (MacIntyre, 1982), and thus when research does not provide direct benefits to the children who participate—even if society benefits—the risk-benefit comparison is a problematic basis for ethical review. Moreover, it is not an easy task to judge the extent of social benefits that are necessary to "balance" meaningful risks to children who participate in research (and who do not enjoy direct benefits from doing so), and this difficulty complicates the comparison of risks and benefits even further.

Moreover, even though both risks and benefits are difficult to estimate, potential benefits are usually harder to predict accurately than are the risks to research participants, especially when benefits are societal in scope. To some extent, this dilemma is inherent in the research process. Risks to research participants can be estimated as soon as research procedures have been designed and study populations selected, but benefits are highly contingent on the outcome of the study and thus involve an estimation of unknowns at the time the research is proposed (this is one justification for conducting the research). Other factors also make benefits difficult to estimate. The social value of research findings often is discovered long after research insights have been generated and are usually contingent on corollary findings, trends in scholarly activity, and the timing of social needs and concerns. Research findings often provide no identifiable social benefits because of unexpected methodological difficulties, resource constraints to continuing the research, or publication obstacles to the dissemination of findings (when prominent journals have formidably high rejection rates). These are problems even when the research is justified solely to advance human knowledge.

For these reasons, comparing risks with benefits in ethical analysis is like comparing apples and oranges. Although the risk-benefit calculus may be a useful heuristic when research of great social importance must be conducted at some essential risk to participants, for most behavioral research it is the comparison of highly uncertain estimates of intangibles. When children are research participants, this comparison is especially problematic because children do not enjoy many of the direct benefits of research participation that adults do, the risks to them are usually greater, and we cannot assume their altruistic motives as research participants. Consequently, the risk-benefit comparison must be combined with normative standards of fair and decent treatment of children as research participants in the ethical review of behavioral research (Thompson, 1990c). Supplementing a threshold analysis of risk-benefit assessment with a prescriptive ethics of treatment norms would make ethical review a graded rather than exclusively a threshold concern, consistent with psychology's commitment to "the preservation and protection of fundamental human rights" and its respect for "the dignity and worth of the individual" (American Psychological Association, 1990), and with ethical responsibilities of nonmaleficence to minimize stresses to children in research, however minor they may be. In this manner, even when research proposals satisfy standards of "minimal risk" or the risk-benefit comparison, researchers remain ethically responsible to the children they study to minimize risks and maximize benefits in whatever ways they can.

Who Should Decide?

In many respects, the inherent indeterminacy of the risk-benefit comparison underscores the importance of who makes these comparative judgments. The identification of possible risks, the delineation of potential benefits, the estimation of the probability of both risks and benefits, and their comparative evaluation each involves complex decision making under conditions of considerable uncertainty. The research literature on judgment and decision making identifies a number of different decisional models that can be applied to these judgments but also indicates that the actual judgments made by decision makers depart significantly from the prescriptions of formal decision models because of the influence of (helpful and misleading) heuristics, biasing factors, presentation of the problem, and inferences concerning the probabilities of various events and their relations to various outcomes, among other factors (Arkes & Hammond, 1986; Pitz & Sachs, 1984). In scientific judgments, as well as in other areas of decision making, the use of intuitive rules of thumb can contribute to misleading, as well as unreliable, judgments (Hammond, Anderson, Sutherland, & Marvin, 1984).

For these reasons, it is wise that decisions concerning the conditions in which a child participates in behavioral research are shared by researchers, parents, and institutional regulators, because the judgments of each party may be misleading taken alone. Researchers are, of course, highly committed to the research activities they pursue and thus are likely to portray their studies as minimally risky and maximally beneficial. Members of IRBs are, in turn, often discouraged from conducting a fine-grained assessment of research risk because of their limited expertise in the specific research field, a reluctance to question their colleagues' ethical competence, and a bias in favor of approval of research protocols (Williams, 1984). Parents, as I have noted, are sometimes unreliable advocates on behalf of their offspring, especially for situations in which they have limited sensitivity to the risks their children may experience (such as those that involve psychological processes of which they are unaware or involve situations that are similar to those they observe frequently at home) or can derive potentially significant benefits from their child's participation in research. Consequently, the convergent judgments of researchers, institutional regulators, and parents concerning the conditions of a child's participation in research are likely to yield the most conservative and protective judgments.

Curiously, however, the child's own consent to research participation seldom enters into this process as a determining influence even though the child is most directly affected by the outcome of this decision. In formulating federal guidelines concerning behavioral research with children, DHHS regulators did not adopt a recommendation of the National Commission that a child's objection to research participation constitute a binding restriction except in extraordinary circumstances, and that the assent of children age 7 and older be required, along with parental permission, for research participation. Pence (1980) has argued that because of the pressures to comply that children commonly experience when their research assent is sought, a child's dissent should be determinative in most research procedures. Instead, however, the DHHS regulations specifically outline the conditions in which research may proceed over a child's manifest objections, and procedures for assuring the child's assent are not strong (Koocher & Keith-Spiegel, 1990).

Clearly, the most formidable challenge in enlisting the child's preferences into the matrix of judgments related to that child's research participation is determining the age at which children are capable of reasoned consent. Obviously, infants and very young children cannot capably understand the research process and rationally consent to their participation, and this lack has led to a spirited philosophical debate concerning whether their participation in research is ever ethically permissible even under conditions of proxy consent by parents (see McCormick, 1974, 1976; Ramsay, 1970, 1976, 1977). On the other hand, most developmental researchers agree that the judgments of children age 11 to 13 in these situations are not substantially different from those of most adults and that this should constitute a minimum age for which children's consent to participate in research is mandatory (e.g., Moshman, 1989; Weithorn, 1982, 1983). Others would argue for a minimum age of 6 to 7, consistent with the recommendations of the National Commission (see Koocher & Keith-Spiegel, 1990; Pence, 1980).

Perhaps searching for a minimum threshold age for children's consent is asking the wrong question. Depending on the context and the complexity of the judgment, children at most ages are capable of making decisions concerning what they want to do, so perhaps the child's competency to consent to research participation should not be regarded as an inflexible limitation deriving from the child's age, but rather as an interaction of the child, the context, and the nature of the (decision-making) task. Children from a surprisingly early age can understand basic elements of the research process and their role within it if this information is presented in an age-appropriate manner, and in such conditions their consent to participate should perhaps be regarded as ethically necessary (even if not sufficient) for them to become involved. The systematic use of alternative consent procedures (such as the use of simplified language, videotaped materials, storybook and illustrated instructions, and presentations by parents or teachers at home or in school; see chapter 7) is likely to lower dramatically the age at which meaningful consent can be obtained from young children. Use of these procedures would have the beneficial outcome of making the consent procedure a shared decision by parent and child and would expand researchers' ethical responsibilities to include providing suitable information and obtaining meaningful consent even from young children who participate in their research. Such an approach is significantly better than the prevailing practice that provides maximal threshold ages (such as age 18) prior to which children's assent to research participation remains optional, not mandatory.

Enfranchising children into the judgment processes regarding their research participation may be beneficial not only for ethical reasons, but also because in so doing, children become more willing, involved, and interested research participants. Thus, as in several other domains of ethical responsibility considered in this analysis, fidelity to ethical responsibility may provide added benefits for the validity of research data as well.

Conclusion

The view of this analysis that the ethical responsibilities of researchers to the children who participate in their studies varies complexly with the child's age and characteristics is not strikingly new, but its implications have important consequences for the ethical review process. If institutional regulators possess inadequate expertise to conduct a sensitive analysis of research risks and benefits with various developmental populations, the ethical review process is undermined by misinformed judgments and misleading guidelines to researchers. This undermining is especially true if, as recommended here, the risk-benefit analysis is supplemented by fidelity to underlying norms concerning the treatment of minors who participate in behavioral research. In light of the enhanced complexity of the ethical review process foreshadowed by this analysis, what is an IRB to do?

Clearly, the professionals who *can* claim pertinent expertise are researchers themselves, so perhaps one recommendation from this analysis is the greater use of developmental researchers in the ethical review process. This could be accomplished through the increased use of developmental experts as invited consultants in the research review process, as well as requiring greater and more detailed information from researchers themselves concerning the psychological consequences of the procedures they propose and the vulnerabilities of the population under study. Moreover, enlisting developmental scholars into the ethical review process also enhances the possibility that this review can be conducted in a collegial, rather than adversarial, manner. Researchers, who are skilled at methodological critique, can enlist these skills in the design of new procedures that may be less risky than those initially envisioned, while also educating IRB members concerning relevant (and irrelevant) domains of potential risk to children of various ages meriting their attention. Different IRB panels might also be composed of experts who specialize in different research domains, with a panel specifically concerned with behavioral research involving minors.

None of these considerations can change the fact that, because of ethical considerations, research is a limited knowledge-acquisition tool. The limitations accepted by researchers because of their ethical responsibilities to research participants can at times have profound implications for the generalizability, validity, and quality of the data they gather (see Weinberger, Tublin, Ford, & Feldman, 1990, for an example). Yet their acceptance of these limitations reveals the underlying humanistic values guiding their scientific enterprise.

References

Aber, J. L., & Cicchetti, D. (1984). The socio-emotional development of maltreated children: An empirical and theoretical analysis. In H. E. Fitzgerald, B. M. Lester, & M. W. Yogman (Eds.), *Theory and research in behavioral pediatrics* (Vol. 2, pp. 147-205). New York: Plenum.

American Psychological Association. (1990). Ethical principles of psychologists. *American Psychologist, 45,* 390-395.

Arkes, H. R., & Hammond, K. R. (1986). General introduction. In H. R. Arkes & K. R. Hammond (Eds.), *Judgment and decision making* (pp. 1-10). Cambridge, UK: Cambridge University Press.

Bartholome, W. G. (1976, December). Parents, children, and the moral benefits of research. *Hastings Center Report,* pp. 44-45.

Baumrind, D. (1978). Reciprocal rights and responsibilities in parent-child relations. *Journal of Social Issues, 34,* 179-196.

Belotti v. Baird, 443 U.S. 662 (1979).

Campos, J. J., Barrett, K. C., Lamb, M. E., Goldsmith, H. H., & Stenberg, C. (1983). Socioemotional development. In M. M. Haith & J. J. Campos (Eds.), P. H. Mussen (Series Ed.), *Handbook of child psychology: Vol. II. Infancy and developmental psychobiology* (pp. 783-915). New York: John Wiley.

Cicchetti, D. (1990). The organization and coherence of socioemotional, cognitive, and representational development: Illustrations through a developmental psychopathology perspective on Down syndrome and child maltreatment. In R. A. Thompson (Ed.), *Socioemotional development. Nebraska Symposium on Motivation, Vol. 36* (pp. 259-366). Lincoln: University of Nebraska Press.

Coleman, J. C. (1980). *The nature of adolescence.* New York: Methuen.

Committee for Ethical Conduct in Child Development Research, Society for Research in Child Development. (1990). SRCD ethical standards for research with children. *SRCD Newsletter, Winter,* 5-7.

Damon, W. (1977). *The social world of the child.* San Francisco: Jossey-Bass.

Damon, W., & Hart, D. (1982). The development of self-understanding from infancy through adolescence. *Child Development, 53,* 841-864.

Department of Health and Human Services (DHHS). (1983). *Protection of human subjects code of federal regulations* 45 CFR 46, Subparts A and D. Washington, DC: Government Printing Office.

Dweck, C. S., & Elliot, E. S. (1983). Achievement motivation. In E. M. Hetherington (Ed.), P. H. Mussen (Series Ed.), *Handbook of child psychology: Vol. IV. Socialization, personality, and social development* (pp. 643-691). New York: John Wiley.

Elkind, D. (1967). Egocentrism in adolescence. *Child Development, 38,* 1025-1033.

Fincham, F. D., & Cain, K. M. (1986). Learned helplessness in humans: A developmental analysis. *Developmental Review, 6,* 301-333.

Fisher, C. B., & Brennan, M. (in press). Application and ethics in developmental psychology. In D. Featherman, R. M. Lerner, & M. Perlmutter (Eds.), *Life-span development and behavior.* New York: Academic Press.

Fisher, C. B., & Rosendahl, S. (in press). Psychological risks and remedies of research participation. In C. B. Fisher & W. W. Tryon (Eds.), *Ethics in applied developmental psychology.* Norwood, NJ: Ablex.

Graham, S., Doubleday, C., & Guarino, P. A. (1984). The development of relations between perceived controllability and the emotions of pity, anger, and guilt. *Child Development, 55,* 561-565.

Grisso, T. (1981). *Juveniles' waiver of rights: Legal and psychological competence.* New York: Plenum.

Hammond, K. R., Anderson, B. F., Sutherland, J., & Marvin, B. (1984). Improving scientists' judgments of risk. *Risk Analysis, 4,* 69-78.

Harter, S. (1983). Developmental perspectives on the self-system. In E. M. Hetherington (Ed.), P. H. Mussen (Series Ed.), *Handbook of child psychology: Vol. IV. Socialization, personality, and social development* (pp. 275-385). New York: John Wiley.

Holder, A. R. (1988). Constraints on experimentation: Protecting children to death. *Yale Law and Policy Review, 6,* 137-156.

Kant, I. (1959). *Foundations of the metaphysics of morals.* New York: Macmillan. (Original work published 1785)

Koocher, G. P., & Keith-Spiegel, P. C. (1990). *Children, ethics, and the law.* Lincoln: University of Nebraska Press.

Kopp, C. B. (1989). Regulation of distress and negative emotions: A developmental view. *Developmental Psychology, 25,* 343-354.

Maccoby, E. E. (1983). Social-emotional development and response to stressors. In N. Garmezy & M. Rutter (Eds.), *Stress, coping, and development in children* (pp. 217-234). New York: McGray-Hill.

MacIntyre, A. (1982). Risk, harm, and benefit assessments as instruments of moral evaluation. In T. L. Beauchamp, R. R. Faden, R. J. Wallace, Jr., & L. Walters (Eds.), *Ethical issues in social science research* (pp. 175-189). Baltimore: Johns Hopkins University Press.

Macklin, R. (1982). The problem of adequate disclosure in social science research. In T. L. Beauchamp, R. R. Faden, R. J. Wallace, Jr., & L. Walters (Eds.), *Ethical issues in social science research* (pp. 193-214). Baltimore: Johns Hopkins University Press.

McCormick, R. A. (1974). Proxy consent in the experimental situation. *Perspectives in Biology and Medicine, 18,* 2-20.

McCormick, R. A. (1976, December). Experimentation in children: Sharing in sociality. *Hastings Center Report,* pp. 41-46.

Meerum Terwogt, M., & Olthof, T. (1989). Awareness and self-regulation of emotion in young children. In C. Saarni & P. L. Harris (Eds.), *Children's understanding of emotion* (pp. 209-237). Cambridge, UK: Cambridge University Press.

Melton, G. B. (1983). Minors and privacy: Are legal and psychological concepts compatible? *Nebraska Law Review, 62,* 455-493.

Melton, G. B. (1987). The clashing of symbols: Prelude to child and family policy. *American Psychologist, 42,* 345-354.

Moshman, D. (1989). *Children, education, and the First Amendment.* Lincoln: University of Nebraska Press.

National Commission for the Protection of Human Subjects of Biomedical and Behavioral Research (NCPHS). (1978). *Research involving children.* Washington, DC: Government Printing Office.

National Commission for the Protection of Human Subjects of Biomedical and Behavioral Research (NCPHS). (1979). *The Belmont report.* Washington, DC: Government Printing Office.

Nicholls, J. G. (1978). The development of the concepts of effort and ability, perception of academic attainment, and the understanding that difficult tasks require more ability. *Child Development, 49,* 800-814.

Pence, G. E. (1980). Children's dissent to research—A minor matter? *IRB: A review of human subjects research, 2,* 1-4.

Piaget, J. (1965). *The moral judgment of the child* (M. Gabain, Trans.). New York: Free Press. (Original work published 1932)

Pitz, G. F., & Sachs, N. J. (1984). Judgment and decision: Theory and application. *Annual Review of Psychology, 35,* 139-163.

Ramsay, P. (1970). *The patient as person.* New Haven, CT: Yale University Press.

Ramsay, P. (1976, August). The enforcement of morals: Nontherapeutic research on children. *Hastings Center Report, pp. 21-30.*

Ramsay, P. (1977, April). Children as research subjects: A reply. *Hastings Center Report, pp. 40-42.*

Ruble, D. N. (1983). The development of social-comparison processes and their role in achievement-related self-socialization. In E. T. Higgins, D. N. Ruble, & W. W. Hartup (Eds.), *Social cognition and social development* (pp. 143-157). Cambridge, UK: Cambridge University Press.

Shantz, C. U. (1983). Social cognition. In J. H. Flavell & E. M. Markman (Eds.), P. H. Mussen (Series Ed.), *Handbook of child psychology: Vol. III. Cognitive development* (pp. 495-555). New York: John Wiley.

Thompson, R. A. (1987). Development of children's inferences of the emotions of others. *Developmental Psychology, 23,* 124-131.

Thompson, R. A. (1988). The effects of infant day care through the prism of attachment theory: A critical appraisal. *Early Childhood Research Quarterly, 3,* 273-282.

Thompson, R. A. (1990a). Attachment theory and research. In M. Lewis (Ed.), *Child and adolescent psychiatry: A comprehensive textbook* (pp. 100-108). Baltimore, MD: Williams & Wilkins.

Thompson, R. A. (1990b). Emotion and self-regulation. In R. A. Thompson (Ed.), *Socioemotional development. Nebraska Symposium on Motivation, Vol. 36* (pp. 383-483). Lincoln: University of Nebraska Press.

Thompson, R. A. (1990c). Vulnerability in research: A developmental perspective on research risk. *Child Development, 61,* 1-16.

Thompson, R. A. & Jacobs, J. (in press). Defining psychological maltreatment: Research and policy perspectives. *Development and Psychopathology,* in press.

Weinberger, D. A., Tublin, S. K., Ford, M. E., & Feldman, S. S. (1990). Preadolescents' social-emotional adjustment and selective attrition in family research. *Child Development, 61,* 1374-1386.

Weithorn, L. A. (1982). Developmental factors and competence to make informed treatment decisions. In G. B. Melton (Ed.), *Legal reforms affecting child and youth services* (pp. 85-100). New York: Haworth.

Weithorn, L. A. (1983). Children's capacities to decide about participation in research. *IRB: A review of human subjects research, 5,* 1-5.

Williams, P. C. (1984). Why IRBs falter in reviewing risks and benefits. *IRB: A review of human subjects research, 6,* 1-4.

Wolfe, M. (1978). Childhood and privacy. In I. Altman & J. F. Wohlwill (Eds.), *Children and the environment* (pp. 175-222). New York: Plenum.

4

Respecting Boundaries

Minors, Privacy, and Behavioral Research

GARY B. MELTON

I often have found that the significance of subtle legal concepts can be explained best through analogous colloquialisms. For example, the threats to due process that are raised by attempts to limit the scope of the confrontation clause of the Sixth Amendment (e.g., provisions for separation of defendants from victim-witnesses in criminal child abuse cases) become meaningful when it is translated "Say it to my face!" Privacy may be best described in similar terms: "Stay out of my space!"

I use this metaphor because the concept of privacy is consensually recognized as having substantial personal and social significance. Invasions of privacy are certainly affectively charged for children as well as adults, as any parent of a primary-grade youngster with a KEEP OUT!!! sign on the bedroom door can attest. Whenever privacy is invaded, the communicated message is that the individual who is the subject[1] of the intrusion is not be taken seriously. One need not undertake a sophisticated ethical or legal analysis to know that an invasion of privacy is degrading; it is *experienced* as a personal violation.

Assuming then that privacy is a matter of importance in everyday life (see Melton, 1988a), including research that purports to present risks no greater than those in everyday life, the problem becomes one of recognizing when a risk of invasion of privacy is present. In common parlance, privacy is "I know when I see it," an elusive construct that has unclear and probably idiosyncratic limits. Indeed, privacy (more precisely, invasions thereof) may be described better as "I know when I *feel* it." A gut sense of personal violation may be the tie that binds such disparate events as being subjected to a body search, being the subject of gossip, having one's mail read, being asked one's income, or having one's house entered without permission. It should come as no surprise that such an intensely personal construct is difficult to define.

Privacy is not just a personal matter, though. Its assertion, whether direct or tacit, is also social, and it is not difficult to imagine situations in which the boundaries of personal space are diffuse or overlapping. Consider again the KEEP OUT!!! sign on a third-grader's bedroom door. The child experiences the room, the possessions in it, and the ideas that they represent or the information that they contain as her own. Her room is the place where the child goes when she "needs some space." In a sense it defines or, at a minimum, reflects the child's identity. Nonetheless, the child's parents are likely to identify the room and its contents as part of *their* space and to experience an intrusion if a person who is not a member of the family enters it or searches its contents without their permission. In fact, they may regard the child as lacking the competence or the authority to control who enters the room and the level of freedom of exploration that visitors have within it (cf. *United States v. Matlock,* 1974).

When the privacy of information (rather than personal territory) is at stake, the situation is likely to be even more confusing. For example, a child asked to write a detailed essay describing "how I spent my summer vacation" may find the topic an invasion of his privacy because of the implicit request for information about his associations and preferences for spending leisure time. Even if not, his parents may view the request as intruding into private family matters (consider, e.g., the situation in which the child spends the summer commuting between divorced parents), but the teacher may see the assignment as an "innocuous"[2] task comporting with the state-sanctioned goal of increasing the child's communication skills.

In short, common experience tells us that privacy is a subjectively important, even critical, aspect of our lives, a point illustrated in recent years in the public debate surrounding the attempt to confirm Robert Bork as a Supreme Court justice. At the same time, though, privacy is a difficult concept to grasp. The matter is especially unclear when children are involved, because they often are viewed as really not worth taking seriously and because their personal privacy often overlaps and sometimes conflicts with family privacy, which in turn often overlaps and sometimes conflicts with the state's interest in child welfare.

I have made these introductory comments as the foundation for two points. First, unsurprisingly, the law of privacy is complex and confusing; one might even say, muddled. Second, it is easy for researchers to be cavalier about private matters, particularly when children are involved. Even when researchers are making a good-faith effort to protect participants' interests, they may be insensitive to the marginal intrusiveness of the research procedures into the personal lives of the participants and/or their families. Particular topics, procedures, or sites for research may have special personal significance that is not identified by researchers convinced of the social good that will arise from their studies and lacking knowledge of the idiosyncratic desires and concerns of participants and their families.

Privacy as a Legal Construct Applied to Adults

A comprehensive discussion of privacy in law is well beyond the scope of this chapter. It is useful to note, though, that its evolution as an important but ambiguous legal construct parallels my introductory discussion. Its significance began to be noted about a century ago in an oft-cited article by Justice-to-be Louis Brandeis and his law partner (Warren & Brandeis, 1890), who were concerned by unseemly and, in their view, unjustified and personally offensive yellow journalism that featured *National Enquirer*-style gossip about prominent individuals, including their own families. In a phrase that subsequently echoed through his own judicial writing (*Olmstead v. United States*, 1928, dissenting opinion) and scores of other judicial opinions and law review articles, Brandeis provided a succinct, colloquial description of privacy: "the right to be let alone."

Legislators, judges, and legal scholars since have invoked the right to be let alone—to have some space—in a dazzling array of constitutional, common-law, and statutory contexts. Nowhere, though, has the concept been more praised and maligned than in the Supreme Court's construction of the constitutional right to privacy, first announced in *Griswold v. Connecticut* (1965). Writing for the majority in *Griswold*,

Justice Douglas described privacy as an overarching, "penumbral" concept in the Bill of Rights, even though it is never expressly mentioned there:

> [Previous] cases suggest that specific guarantees in the Bill of Rights have penumbras, formed by emanations from those guarantees that help give them life and substance. . . . Various guarantees create zones of privacy. The right of association contained in the penumbra of the First Amendment is one. . . . The Third Amendment in its prohibition against the quartering of soldiers "in any house" in time of peace without the consent of the owner is another facet of this privacy. The Fourth Amendment explicitly affirms the "right of the people to be secure in their persons, houses, papers, and effects, against unreasonable searches and seizures." The Fifth Amendment in its Self-Incrimination Clause enables the citizen to create a zone of privacy which government may not force him to surrender to his detriment. The Ninth Amendment provides: "The enumeration, in the Constitution, of certain rights, shall not be construed to deny or disparage others retained by the people." (p. 484)

Griswold was extended in *Roe v. Wade* (1973), the most famous application of the right to privacy. The Court did little more in *Roe* to elucidate the meaning of the right to privacy. In the opinion for the Court, Justice Blackmun said simply that the right to privacy has "some relationship" to matters of marriage, reproduction, and family relationships. Although he indicated that the foundation for the right to privacy might be in the substantive due-process clause of the Fourteenth Amendment, Blackmun did little to explicate the difference between privacy and liberty. Of significance to determinations of privacy in matters pertaining to children and families, Blackmun did imply that freedom from government intrusions into family life is subsumed within the right to privacy.[3]

The limits of the right to privacy have been unclear, with the Supreme Court having given a mixed message even about the application of the right to diverse sexual relationships (*Bowers v. Hardwick*, 1986) and with the right to privacy in abortion decisions perilously close to being overruled (*Webster v. Reproductive Health Services*, 1989). Some lower courts have extended the right, though, at least to other contexts involving family matters or protection of bodily integrity (see, e.g., *Merriken v. Cressman*, 1973, discussed infra; *Rogers v. Okin*, 1980).

Privacy as a Legal Construct Applied to Minors

Supreme Court Cases

Adolescent abortion. The jurisprudence of the right to privacy as applied to minors parallels the adult cases, but it does so with ambivalence and even greater unclarity. In a series of cases testing the constitutionality of states' restrictions on adolescents' access to abortion and contraception, the Supreme Court has recognized that minors, as persons, are entitled to protection of privacy in reproductive decisions. This principle was stated most unequivocally in the first of the cases, *Planned Parenthood of Central Missouri v. Danforth* (1976), in which Justice Blackmun wrote the opinion for a sharply divided Court. Even in *Danforth,* though, the Court indicated that limits exist on minors' right to privacy that are not present for adults. Besides suggesting that the right to privacy would be recognized only for *mature* minors, the Court stacked the deck against minors' expression of the right to privacy by implying that such a right could be abrogated by a showing merely of a contrary *significant* state interest.[4]

In subsequent adolescent abortion cases, the Court has devoted much more attention to the reasons that minors' right to privacy may be infringed than to the need for protecting such a right. In *Bellotti v. Baird* (1979), the Court cited three reasons for imposing such limitations: minors' "inability to make critical decisions in an informed, mature manner," their "peculiar vulnerability," and the need to protect the integrity of the family. Despite substantial contrary evidence (Melton, 1986, 1987b), the Court consistently has discovered incompetence, vulnerability, and dependency sufficient to limit adolescents' privacy in abortion decisions in ways that the Court has held unconstitutional when applied to adults.

School searches. The Court has been similarly ambivalent in other legal contexts involving minors' privacy. In *New Jersey v. T. L. O.* (1985), the Court considered the applicability of the Fourth Amendment to public school students. Writing for the majority, Justice White began by acknowledging that it is "indisputable . . . that the Fourteenth Amendment protects the rights of students against encroachment by public school officials" (p. 334), indeed that a search of a student's handbag or person is "undoubtedly a severe violation of subjective expectations of privacy" (p. 338). The Court noted that high school students frequently carry "the necessaries of personal hygiene and grooming," as well as "such nondisruptive yet highly personal items as photographs, letters, and diaries" (p. 339).

Even with such apparently forthright acknowledgment of students' legitimate expectations of privacy, the Court clearly felt some discomfort. Refusing to apply the standard of virtual absence of legitimate expectations of privacy that the Court had established recently in a prison case (*Hudson v. Palmer,* 1984), the Court remarkably found it necessary to state that "[w]e are not yet ready to hold that the schools and the prisons need be equated for purposes of the Fourth Amendment" (*New Jersey v. T. L. O.,* 1985 p. 338-339). Two justices in the majority (Powell and O'Connor) made clear in a concurring opinion that at least they believed that students' expectations of privacy are diminished substantially in the school setting.

In a decision that has been roundly criticized by scholarly commentators (e.g., Gardner, 1988), the Court ultimately held in *T. L. O.* that a warrantless search by school officials could be justified merely by reasonable suspicion of violation of a school rule. Joined by Justices Brennan and Marshall in a partial dissent, Justice Stevens ascerbically observed that, "[f]or the Court, a search for curlers and sunglasses in order to enforce the school dress code is apparently just as important as a search for evidence of heroin addiction or violent gang activity" (p. 377).

The dissenters also doubted that the reasonable suspicion standard offered any protection of privacy at all:

> The majority's application of its standard in this case—to permit a male administrator to rummage through the purse of a female high school student in order to obtain evidence that she was smoking in a bathroom—raises grave doubts in my mind whether its effort will be effective. (p. 381)

The Court's crabbed view of minors' personhood is not unique to *T. L. O.* In recent years, the Court has had a pattern in children's rights cases of briefly acknowledging that a constitutionally protected interest is at stake and then launching into a lengthy discourse about why the interest needs little protection (see, e.g., *Parham v. J. R.,* 1979). Similarly, the Court has resurrected the argument that juvenile detention is not a very serious matter because juveniles' interest in liberty "must be qualified by the recognition that juveniles, unlike adults, are always in some form of custody" (*Schall v. Martin,* 1984, p. 265).

Cases in Other Courts

School searches. The Supreme Court's narrow view of the significance of privacy to minors is not an idiosyncracy of the aged members of the Court.[5] Some lower courts had viewed the meaningfulness
of the concept with even more skepticism, especially in search-and-
seizure law.

For example, in language that makes *T.L.O.* appear benign but that
was approved by the Seventh Circuit Court of Appeals (prior to the
Supreme Court's decision in *T.L.O.*), an Indiana federal district court
sanctioned a canine search for drugs of all junior and senior high
school students in one school district:

> Students are exposed to various intrusions into their classroom environ-
> ment. The presence of the canine team for several minutes was a minimal
> intrusion at best and not so serious as to invoke the protections of the
> Fourth Amendment. . . .
>
> Any expectation of privacy necessarily diminishes in light of a student's
> constant supervision while in school. Because of the constant interaction
> among student, faculty and school administrators, a public school student
> cannot be said to enjoy any absolute expectation of privacy while in the
> classroom setting. (*Doe v. Renfrow,* 1979, pp. 1020-1022, citation omitted)

Compounding this demeaning view of schoolchildren was District
Judge Sharp's incredible finding of fact that "[n]o incidents of disrup-
tion occurred in the classrooms because of the presence of the dogs or
the teams" (*Doe v. Renfrow,* 1979, p. 1017). This purportedly ordinary school day included the arrival of the canine teams (complete
with the press and the police), locking of the doors, a sniff-search of
each pupil, and when the dog "alerted" (always falsely, as it turned
out), a search of the pupil's pockets or purse, a body search, and even
a strip search.

Judge Sharp's rather bizarre view of reality apparently arose from
his desire to support "a group of dedicated people [school administra-
tors] who carry heavy legal and moral obligations for public education" (*Doe v. Renfrow,* 1979, p. 1026). Such a denial of children's
experience in order to justify a particular legal order is hardly unique
to Judge Sharp (see Melton, 1987a). Nonetheless, the important consequences of intrusions on the privacy of children and youth are ob-
scured, as Justice Brennan recognized in his solitary dissent from

the Supreme Court's denial of certiorari (refusal to hear the case) in *Renfrow:*

> We do not know what class petitioner was attending when the police and dogs burst in, but the lesson the school authorities taught her that day will undoubtedly make a greater impression than the one her teacher had hoped to convey. I would grant certiorari to teach petitioner another lesson: that the Fourth Amendment protects "[t]he right of the people to be secure in their persons, houses, papers, and effects, against unreasonable searches and seizures," and that before police and local officers are permitted to conduct dog-assisted dragnet inspections of public school students, they must obtain a warrant based on sufficient particularized evidence to establish probable cause to believe a crime has been or is being committed. Schools cannot expect their students to learn the lessons of good citizenship when the school authorities themselves disregard the fundamental principles underpinning our constitutional freedoms. (*Doe v. Renfrow*, 1981, pp. 1027-1028)

Merriken v. Cressman. The reported case most directly germane to the question of minors' privacy in research was *Merriken vs. Cressman* (1973), indeed the only reported case of "malresearch" in the social sciences. In *Merriken,* a Pennsylvania school district launched an experimental program to reduce drug abuse. The program included administration of a personality test purported to identify potential drug abusers, followed by various compulsory interventions, including confrontational group therapy programs, for those who met the screening criteria. The testing program was intended to create a "massive data bank" for use by "superintendents, principals, guidance counselors, athletic coaches, social workers, PTA officers, and school board members" (p. 916). Parental permission originally was sought only through a passive "book-of-the-month club" procedure. After the suit was filed, "affirmative written parental consent" was sought but without disclosure of the risks associated with the program. Student consent or assent initially was not sought at all although the procedure ultimately was revised to permit submission of blank questionnaires.

Although the court acknowledged that youth themselves have a fundamental right to privacy, it stopped short of deciding the case in such terms. Instead, the court found that the petitioner's mother had suffered an invasion of *her* constitutional right to privacy because the personality test included "such personal and private questions as the family religion, the race or skin color of the student . . . the family composition, including the reason for the absence of one or both parents, and whether one or both parents 'hugged and kissed me when I was small,' 'tell me how much they love me,' 'enjoyed talking about current events with me,' and 'make me feel unloved' " (p. 916).

Merriken thus illustrates the way in which behavioral research involving children and youth can infringe the privacy rights of third parties (e.g., parents), as well as children themselves. It also shows the degree of intrusiveness that accompanies commonly used behavioral research techniques (e.g., paper-and-pencil personality tests). Whether nonconsensual research of such a sort necessarily involves constitutionally protected interests, though, should be regarded as unsettled. *Merriken* is low-level authority (a federal district court decision), and it was decided well before the recent spate of cases calling into question the scope of the constitutional right to privacy.

The Psychology of Privacy

Elements of Privacy

As the discussion of the law of privacy, privacy is an enormously complex and quite fuzzy concept unified only by a concern with the integrity of personal boundaries. To understand the contours of privacy, it is useful to differentiate dimensions underlying the concept. Laufer and Wolfe (1977) described three dimensions of privacy that may vary systematically across privacy experiences: self-ego dimension (privacy in the context of personal individuation); environmental dimension (elements of the social context, including "cultural meanings, the interaction between the social arrangements and the physical settings, and the stage of the life cycle"; p. 28), and interpersonal dimension ("[p]rivacy, in whatever form, presupposes the existence of others and the possibility of a relationship with them"; p. 33). The Laufer-Wolfe conceptualization is useful for further research on privacy because it calls attention to both interpersonal and phenomenological aspects of experiences of privacy.

I (Melton, 1983) have offered a conceptualization of dimensions of privacy based on the nature of the "zones" or interests protected: bodily privacy, management of access to personal space, and management of access to personal information. Although not as rich as the Laufer-Wolfe formulation for understanding the psychology of privacy, it is useful for policy analysis and related research because the dimensions that I have noted are analogous to foci of legal protection.

The Developmental Significance of Privacy

The only general developmental study of concepts of privacy was conducted by Wolfe (1978), who interviewed 900 children and adolescents ages 5 to 17. Wolfe and her colleagues also have examined the significance of privacy in various special settings (e.g., institutions; Rivlin & Wolfe, 1985). The only other study specifically of privacy in childhood was of territorial privacy practices among middle-class families (Parke & Sawin, 1979).

These studies indicate that privacy is salient even for primary schoolchildren. As might be expected, though, the psychological components of privacy change with age. As children become older, expression of privacy becomes an active choice, with their being less subject to intrusion on their "private" space, associations, and information. Privacy has a particularly important meaning to adolescents as a marker of independence and self-differentiation. Although "being alone" is an important element of privacy to adolescents as it is to younger children, adolescents also find maintenance of control over personal information to be particularly critical. As I have phrased it elsewhere, "Such control denotes respect for the dignity and personhood of the adolescent; it provides the opportunity for the development of intimate relationships and recognition that the adolescent now faces decisions which in our culture are marked as 'private' and belonging to the individual" (Melton, 1983, pp. 488-489).

Further evidence for the importance of privacy to children and youth is given by empirical studies of experiences of degradation and personal violation in childhood. Children evaluate the quality of living situations by the degree of invasion of privacy and infringement of liberty present within them (see, e.g., Bush, 1980; Rivlin & Wolfe, 1985; Roth & Roth, 1984). Similarly, elementary-school-age children describe threats to their personal integrity (e.g., accusations of lying) as among the most stressful events that they do or might experience (Yamamoto, 1979).[6]

Indeed, psychological research and theory on the significance of privacy for the maintenance of self-esteem and development of personal identity is remarkable for its congruence with legal and philosophical discourse on the relation of privacy to human dignity (Melton, 1983; Tremper, 1988; Tremper & Kelly, 1987). In that sense, it serves as a model for the utility of a psychological approach to jurisprudence (see Melton, 1990; Melton & Saks, 1985).

Principles for the Ethical Consideration of Privacy in Research

When an ethical framework is applied to the lessons from common experience, law, and psychology, several principles emerge for the protection of privacy in child development research. These principles are generally consonant with those expressly stated in the federal regulations governing research and the ethical standards of the social science professions, but they may exceed the letter if not the spirit of the current regulations and standards.

The privacy interests of both children and their families are serious matters deserving great weight in decisions about whether and how to conduct research involving them.

Protection of privacy signals respect for the integrity of children as autonomous persons and families as fundamental social units in which individuals forge their most intimate relationships. Therefore, any invasion of privacy wrongs the subject, regardless of its consequences, because it violates the individual's personhood.

Nonetheless, the evidence for the importance of privacy in the development of the self-esteem of children and the identity of adolescents implies that invasions of privacy also create harm. When an invasion of privacy also subjects children to embarrassment or shame through disclosure of intimate information, the harm is multiplied. Accordingly, the principle of beneficence also demands respect for privacy.

As a general rule, the more deeply private an experience or behavior is, the more careful researchers should be to protect it.

Some topics or behavior are so intensely private that any intrusion is simply indecent. No matter what the motives of the intruder, the infringement of privacy is experienced as a personal violation. For example, Small (1988; Small & Wiener, in press) found that citizens regarded any monitoring of dressing rooms as unacceptable even though they were willing to tolerate other forms of surveillance to deter or uncover illicit behavior. Interestingly, personality testing evoked a reaction almost as intense in Small's door-to-door survey of adult respondents.

Although research on the point is lacking, it is probable that the range of inherently abhorrent intrusions is broader for children and adolescents than for adults because of the acute meaning of privacy in personality development. For example, use of genital plethysmographs might be considered unduly intrusive in any research with adolescents because of the fragility of sexual self-esteem as it develops, even if the procedure is acceptable with consenting adult participants in legitimate research on sexuality.

Participants' consent should be obtained before a zone of privacy is invaded.

At its root, privacy involves control over personal boundaries. Therefore, a violation of personal dignity—a wrong—necessarily occurs unless the intrusion is consensual. This general principle applies, of course, regardless of the nature of the specific privacy interest at stake.

Procedures should be no more intrusive than necessary to obtain information about the phenomena under study.

Even if consensual, invasions of privacy should not occur if a less intrusive means of generating knowledge about a particular phenomenon is available. Gratuitous or thoughtless invasions of privacy are at best cavalier and at worst voyeuristic exploitation of participants anxious to contribute to social welfare. Overly intrusive research procedures signal that *participants* are being used as *subjects* who are not taken seriously.

The least-intrusive-means principle applies throughout the research process. For example, sampling procedures should minimize possible embarrassment to potential participants. Researchers also must be mindful of this principle in deciding when and where to collect data and in judging the degree of acceptable physical and psychological invasiveness of the research procedures themselves. Personal questions that are potentially interesting but that are essentially gratuitous in the context of the primary goals of a given research project should not be included in interview protocols or paper-and-pencil surveys.

Insensitivity to the intrusiveness of research procedures may be particularly common in research involving children and families. As I have already discussed, this callousness may result from the denigration of the significance of privacy to children, but I suspect that the process may be more subtle. Psychologists often are desensitized to talking about personal matters (especially *other* people's private lives), and it is easy to forget that many people find questions about

their family life to be a bit embarrassing at best and blatantly offensive at worse. Similarly, researchers performing home observations of
parent-child interaction may give insufficient advance thought to the
physical boundaries that observers will not cross without an affirmative invitation from the participants/hosts.

**Care should be taken to ensure that information given in confi-
dence remains so.**

Although the norms about protection of personal space may not be
well settled in the health sciences, the general duty to protect confidentiality of personal information is known widely and probably respected widely. Thus, psychologists, for example, have a "primary
obligation" to guard clients' and research participants' control over
personal information (American Psychological Association, 1981,
Principle 5; see also Principle 9j). However, this norm may not be so
consensually held in sensitive research involving minors.

Some of the uncertainty and controversy is unique to research involving minors. As Mulvey and Phelps (1988) summarized:

> Decisions about . . . [maintenance of confidentiality] are complicated in the
> case of juveniles because juveniles are not fully autonomous individuals in
> the eyes of either their communities or their parents, and the interests of
> both the family and the community must figure into the calculation of the
> limits of the confidentiality contract. The community has a justifiable stake
> in fostering the development of responsible citizens and in maintaining
> public safety; the family has a privacy interest in raising children according
> to its own standards, rather than those of therapeutic professionals or state
> agencies. The confidentiality issue becomes troublesome when the profes-
> sional possesses information that would be seen by either of these parties as
> essential to their professional role. The basic difficulty in these cases lies in
> the professional's felt sense of responsibility for pursuing the youth's best
> interest or for honoring privacy rights and placing the burden for interven-
> tion on other parties involved with the youth. (p. 66)

Note that these issues are present even if one assumes the interests
of parents and state authorities to be congruent with those of youth
themselves. If parents are concerned with their children's well-being
not because (or not solely because) of their interest in promoting a
particular form of socialization but instead because of their societally
recognized duty to protect dependent youth, that duty sometimes cannot be fulfilled without access to information that their children
would prefer to keep from them.

For that reason, although clinicians generally have no legal duty to warn relatives about a client's self-destructive potential (*Bellah v. Greenson,* 1978), it is arguable that the special relationship between client and therapist extends to a minor client's parents so that disclosure is required when the clinician believes the client to be self-destructive (see Melton, 1989). If such a duty is applicable to therapists, it is likely in many circumstances also to apply to researchers (Appelbaum & Rosenbaum, 1989).

Although parents and children do not always have coextensive interests, in most instances they share an interest in avoiding state-compelled disclosures of research data to others.[7] Information that is embarrassing to youth also is apt to be viewed by parents as family matters. Disclosure of illegal behavior may result in proceedings that may both disrupt the family and subject parents and/or children to legal penalties.

The Law on Confidentiality of Data

Threats to Confidentiality

Under several circumstances the state may compel breaches of confidentiality (see Gray & Melton, 1985, for a detailed discussion with relevant citations; see also Melton & Gray, 1988). Most broadly, disclosure that is voluntary from the point of view of the researcher but goes beyond the range of disclosure that participants intended may occur under "routine uses." Although the participants may believe that only the researcher and an assistant will view their data in identifiable form, a wide range of agency staff may in fact have access to the data. Moreover, when an external funding agency is involved, staff of that agency may have access to the data for audits and secondary analyses.

Furthermore, once a federal agency has control of the data, they generally will be accessible to the public under the Freedom of Information Act (Morris, Sales, & Berman, 1981). Researchers can best guard against such breaches of confidentiality by insisting on audits on research site without physical surrender of the data.

Most seriously, data may be subpoenaed by litigants or legislative or administrative investigators. Subpoenae are especially pernicious threats to confidentiality. They typically occur for reasons unrelated to the study itself and, therefore, are not reasonably foreseeable by participants. For example, a grand jury sought the records of a sociology graduate student who was conducting a participant-observer study of the sociology of a restaurant when arson occurred there, possibly related to an ongoing labor dispute about which the researcher had knowledge (*In re Grand Jury Subpoena,* 1984). In other instances, pharmaceutical companies involved in product safety litigation have subpoenaed the records of gynecological health registries (*Deitchman v. E. R. Squibb & Sons,* 1984; *Farnsworth v. Procter & Gamble Co.,* 1985; *Lampshire v. Procter & Gamble Co.,* 1982).

Compelled disclosure of data through subpoenae thus can subject participants to substantial harm. As the examples illustrate, when data are subpoenaed, they commonly are especially sensitive, and their disclosure may result in great embarrassment. Moreover, as occurred in *In re Grand Jury Subpoena* (1984), prosecutors or grand juries may seek data expressly as a basis for initiating or pursuing criminal prosecutions (see also Kershaw & Small, 1972). Indeed, in *Merriken v. Cressman* (1973), discussed earlier, the court was concerned that the promise of confidentiality of data was hollow because "an enterprising district attorney [might] convene a special grand jury to investigate the drug problem" and there would then be no assurance that information about self-disclosed drug users would be free from subpoena (p. 916).

Once a subpoena is enforced, the cost to personal dignity is likely to be exacerbated by the fact that the data then typically will be in the public domain. Not only is privacy infringed by the initial compelled disclosure, but that wrong is apt to be repeated many times over.

Protection of Confidentiality

Just as the law may threaten confidentiality, it also may provide protection against unjustified intrusions on privacy. For example, Federal Rule of Civil Procedure 26(c) permits courts to issue "any order which justice requires to protect a party or persons from annoyance, embarrassment, oppression, or undue burden or expense." On a case-by-case basis, courts also may determine that the social costs of chilling of research and embarrassment of participants outweigh the benefit to justice that litigants' access to data will promote (Federal Rule of Evidence 501), although a full disclosure to participants of the risks of invasion of privacy ironically may decrease the applicability of such a common-law privilege (Gray & Melton, 1985).

Given the unpredictability of case-by-case determinations of the enforceability of subpoenae, the best protection that researchers can obtain for the confidentiality of data is a certificate of confidentiality. The most widely applicable authority for such a certificate is contained in the Public Health Service (PHS) Act, as amended by the Health Omnibus Programs Extension of 1988. Under the PHS Act, the Secretary of Health and Human Services may

> authorize persons engaged in biomedical, behavioral, clinical, or other research (including research on mental health, including research on the use and effect of alcohol and other psychoactive drugs), to protect the privacy of individuals who are the subject of such research by withholding from all persons not connected with the conduct of such research the names or other identifying characteristics of such individuals. Persons so authorized to protect the privacy of such individuals may not be compelled in any federal, state, or local civil, criminal, administrative, legislative, or other proceedings to identify such individuals.[8]

The scope of the authority for issuing certificates of confidentiality is broad. Indeed, it is hard to imagine human research outside the range of "biomedical, behavioral, clinical, or other research," and the secretary appears to have no grounds for refusing a certificate (at least prior to the time that the data collection is initiated) other than a finding that the request for a certificate is to cover information other than that involved in bona fide research. For example, the secretary might legitimately refuse to issue a certificate if clinical practice or other work were recast as research simply to obtain a privilege against subpoena.

Nonetheless, the protection offered by the PHS Act is not as tight as it should be—perhaps not as complete as Congress intended.[9] First, because researchers must apply for certificates, the protection that they offer participants is subject to researchers' knowledge and diligence, and there is not principled reason why that should be so. Even among federally funded studies relatively little research producing sensitive data is covered by a certificate because researchers either do not know about the provision, do not foresee a need for a certificate, or simply do not invest the time in obtaining one. Therefore, at least for those branches of the Department of Health and Human Services

(DHHS) that conduct or fund sensitive research (i.e., PHS, the Office of Human Development Services, and their constituent institutes and centers), certificates for funded research should be provided automatically, as in fact is the case under analogous protection offered participants in studies funded by the Department of Justice.[10] If such automatic protection is afforded to participants, researchers in non-federally-funded projects still should be permitted to obtain certificates on a discretionary basis.

Second, the language of the PHS Act is sufficiently imprecise that holes may be found in the protection offered by participants. Because the immunity to subpoena is applied to "names or other identifying characteristics," the data of a known participant are not expressly protected. Although Congress's intent was "to protect the privacy" of participants,[11] the statute might be interpreted not to protect data per se.

For example, in one of my own studies, all of the children in a particular county who are involved in criminal child abuse prosecutions are invited to participate. Knowing that fact, a defense attorney might seek the data of a particular child (not the names of participants) as a fishing expedition for information intended to impeach the child's testimony. A literal interpretation of the statute would suggest that the subpoena might be enforceable if the data could be shown in some way to be relevant to the proceeding. Although it also is possible— perhaps even probable—that a court would interpret the statute more broadly in keeping with congressional intent, the uncertainty prevents unequivocal offers of confidentiality to participants and, therefore, should be eliminated by a technical amendment.[12]

Uncertainty also exists about whether child abuse reporting laws are abrogated by certificates of confidentiality. The answer under the PHS Act as it is worded presently depends on whether such reports are legal "proceedings." This question also should be clarified through legislative amendment.

Whose Interests Are at Stake?

One curiosity of the several reported cases on subpoenae of research data is that participants have been largely absent from the disputes (Cecil & Boruch, 1988; Melton, 1988b). Insofar as courts have attended to participants' reactions to court-compelled disclosure of data that they believed they had given in confidence, the courts have been concerned almost exclusively with the chilling effect of enforced subpoenae—the possibility that subpoenae of data will deter participation in research, especially studies of sensitive topics. In other words, the courts have worried about the effect of subpoenae on *potential* participants, not the participants themselves. Even with regard to the potential participants, the concern really has not been for such individuals but instead for the society as a whole, who would be deprived of their data.

Indeed, courts have appeared to be bothered much more by the adverse effects of breaches of confidentiality on the researchers who (presumably unwittingly) gave false promises to participants of protection of their privacy. Courts have worried that researchers would effectively be deprived of the fruits of their labor without due process because of the cost of premature disclosure of data and concomitant loss of publication opportunities and the economic benefits that accompany them. Researchers' interests have been presumed to be coextensive with society's interests because interference with the research enterprise and loss of economic benefits for researchers might result ultimately in less vigorous pursuit of knowledge.

The apparent lack of legal recognition of participants' privacy interests has reflected the way the cases are framed more than the state of the law protecting participants (Melton, 1988b). Because researchers themselves are the recipients of subpoenae, it is unsurprising that the protection of their interests is the primary concern when courts are deciding whether they must surrender their data. As I have noted already, courts now clearly have the authority under the rules of procedure and evidence to quash or limit subpoenae to protect participants from embarrassment.

Even if courts now have discretion to protect participants' privacy, legal protection of confidentiality is inadequate. Both justice and efficiency demand that researchers expressly be given standing to assert privileges on behalf of participants in their studies (see Melton, 1988b). As Congress apparently intended in the PHS Act and its amendments, an absolute researcher-participant privilege should exist. The arguments actually are stronger for such a privilege than for other privileges that have had historic recognition (e.g., psychotherapist-client privilege), because society already has reaped the benefits of their contribution; in a sense, we have taken advantage of them. I can put the matter no more strongly than in my previous commentary on the subject:

> Failure to respect participants' privacy would be a particularly cruel breach of their trust, because they have, after all, permitted themselves to be *used* in the interest of promoting social good, usually without benefit to themselves. If fidelity to a contract has any moral significance, surely its significance is especially acute when people give of themselves, with expectations only that they be treated with dignity and appropriate protection from harm. . . .
>
> In short, although participants' interests are the least discussed in debates and judicial opinions about access to data, I would place those interests preeminent. Potentially identifiable data about personal matters—probably the majority of psychological research—should not be provided to either courts or secondary researchers without the informed consent of the participants. Legislation to ensure privacy of participants should be adopted, and professional ethical codes should continue to emphasize the "primary obligation" of protection of confidentiality.
>
> When participants have given of themselves to promote knowledge, they should be able to expect that their altruism will not be rewarded with a violation of their dignity or a risk of public humiliation or even legal penalties. Research with human participants, especially on topics of great social import, inherently involves some conflict between individual and social good. In that regard, respect for persons demands that we should take special care to avoid sacrifice or exploitation of individuals in the name of social benefit. (Melton, 1988b, pp. 193, 198, footnotes omitted)

Conclusions

Although these comments were focused on privacy of information, they are applicable to protection of other forms of privacy and indeed to protection of research participants' interests in general. When the determination is made that the balance between good for society and inconvenience or potential harm to participants can be struck reasonably in favor of the former so that a study can be conducted, then we should take care to ensure that the cost to individuals is not compounded. In that regard, those interests most fundamental to protection of human dignity should be given special attention, and surely privacy is among them.

Although the consideration of such issues is more complex when minors are involved, it is no less critical. Respect for human dignity is a useful organizing construct for child policy, just as it is for "adult law" (Tremper, 1988). Indeed, as developmental research and theory indicate, protection of privacy has special significance for older children and adolescents as they develop a differentiated sense of self. If minors' participation in research is to be justified in part by its educational value, then the lesson that is communicated surely should include respect for persons. Just as children should learn the virtues of cooperation and altruism, they should learn that we appreciate such contributions to social good and that, at a minimum, we will take such individuals seriously, as they are taking seriously their duties to the society as a whole.

Notes

1. The use of the term *subject* here is intentional. When research participants are treated as subjects—as means to ends—rather than persons, the significance of privacy is likely to be underestimated.

2. I have put quotation marks around the term *innocuous* because it is the descriptor that social scientists often use to attempt to justify minimal risk, but arguably wrongful research (e.g., deception designs).

3. Three old cases dealing with the limits of government interference with child rearing (*Meyer v. Nebraska,* 1923; *Pierce v. Society of Sisters,* 1925; *Prince v. Massachusetts,* 1944) were cited in *Roe* as part of the authority for the existence of a right to privacy in the Constitution.

4. The fundamental rights of adults (i.e., rights implicitly or expressly contained in the Constitution) may be infringed only when such an intrusion is justified by a *compelling* state interest.

5. Compare *Bethel School District v. Fraser* (1986), in which Justice Stevens prefaced his dissenting opinion by suggesting that a Supreme Court composed of "a group of judges who are at least two generations away" (p. 692) had misjudged the sensibilities of high school students.

6. This finding also suggests that being deceived is unlikely to be viewed by children as a trivial event.

7. I previously have noted instances in which parents and children may have different views about state intrusions on privacy of research data:

> The statutory duty to report child maltreatment is an example of an instance in which parents arguably have a privacy interest that conflicts with that of their children. On the other hand, youth may wish to preserve a zone of privacy around intimate, risky behavior when both the state and the parents believe that their knowledge of such behavior is essential to protection of the youth from harm. (Melton, 1989, p. 415, footnote 4)

8. 42 U.S.C. § 242a(b) (1989).

9. The law reforms proposed here have been endorsed by several governance bodies of the American Psychological Association: for example, the Committee for Protection of Human Participants in Research, the Task Force on Psychology and AIDS, the Division of Child, Youth, and Family Services, and the American Psychology-Law Society.

10. 28 CFR Part 22 (July 1, 1988).

11. 42 U.S.C. § 242a.

12. In the example given, ambiguity may still be found even after resolution of the uncertainty about the scope of the privilege accorded by a certificate of confidentiality. Because any statutory privilege must give way to a constitutionally protected interest, even a crystal clear privilege would be abrogated if the defendant could prove that its application would deprive him or her of the right to due process.

References

American Psychological Association. (1981). Ethical principles of psychologists. *American Psychologist, 36,* 633-638.

Appelbaum, P. S., & Rosenbaum, A. (1989). *Tarasoff* and the researcher: Does the duty to protect apply in the research setting. *American Psychologist, 44,* 885-894.

Bellah v. Greenson, 81 Cal.App.3d 614, 146 Cal. Rptr. 535 (1978).

Bellotti v. Baird, 443 U.S. 622 (1979).

Bethel School District v. Fraser, 478 U.S. 678 (1986).

Bowers v. Hardwick, 478 U.S. 186 (1986).

Bush, M. (1980). Institutions for dependent and neglected children: Therapeutic option of choice or last resort? *American Journal of Orthopsychiatry, 50,* 239-255.

Cecil, J. S., & Boruch, R. F. (1988). Compelled disclosures of research data: An early warning and suggestions for psychologists. *Law and Human Behavior, 12,* 181-189.

Deitchman v. E. R. Squibb & Sons, Inc., 740 F.2d 556 (7th Cir. 1984).

Doe v. Renfrow, 475 F. Supp. 1012 (N.D. Ind. 1979), *aff'd in part, remanded in part,* 631 F.2d 91 (7th Cir. 1980), *reh'g and reh'g en banc denied,* 635 F.2d 582 (7th Cir. 1980), *cert. denied,* 451 U.S. 1022 (1981).

Farnsworth v. Procter & Gamble Co., 758 F.2d 1545 (11th Cir. 1985).

Gardner, M. R. (1988). Student privacy in the wake of *T.L.O.:* An appeal for an individualized suspicion requirement for valid searchers and seizures in the schools. *Georgia Law Review, 22,* 897-947.

Gray, J. N., & Melton, G. B. (1985). The law and ethics of psychosocial research on AIDS. *Nebraska Law Review, 64,* 637-688.

Griswold v. Connecticut, 381 U.S. 479 (1965).

Hudson v. Palmer, 468 U.S. 576 (1984).

In re Grand Jury Subpoena Dated January 4, 1984, 750 F.2d 223 (2d Cir. 1984).

Kershaw, D. N., & Small, J. C. (1972). Data confidentiality and privacy: Lessons from the New Jersey negative income tax experiment. *Public Policy, 20,* 257-280.

Lampshire v. Procter & Gamble Co., 94 F.R.D. 58 (N.D. Ga. 1982).

Laufer, R. S., & Wolfe, M. (1977). Privacy as a concept and a social issue: A multidimensional developmental theory. *Journal of Social Issues, 33*(3), 22-42.

Melton, G. B. (1983). Minors and privacy: Are legal and psychological concepts compatible? *Nebraska Law Review, 62,* 455-493.

Melton, G. B. (Ed.). (1986). *Adolescent abortion: Psychological and legal issues.* Lincoln: University of Nebraska Press.

Melton, G. B. (1987a). The clashing of symbols: Prelude to child and family policy. *American Psychologist, 42,* 345-354.

Melton, G. B. (1987b). Legal regulation of adolescent abortion: Unintended effects. *American Psychologist, 42,* 79-83.

Melton, G. B. (1988a). The significance of law in the everyday lives of children and families. *Georgia Law Review, 22,* 851-895.

Melton, G. B. (1988b). When scientists are adversaries, do participants lose? *Law and Human Behavior, 12,* 191-198.

Melton, G. B. (1989). Ethical and legal issues in research and intervention [related to AIDS]. *Journal of Adolescent Health Care, 10,* 36S-44S.

Melton, G. B. (1990). Law, science, and humanity: The normative foundation of social science in law. *Law and Human Behavior, 14,* 315-332.

Melton, G. B., & Gray, J. N. (1988). Ethical dilemmas in AIDS research: Individual privacy and public health. *American Psychologist, 43,* 60-64.

Melton, G. B., & Saks, M.J. (1985). The law as an instrument of socialization and social structure. In G. B. Melton (Ed.), *Nebraska Symposium on Motivation: Vol. 33. The law as a behavioral instrument* (pp. 235-277). Lincoln: University of Nebraska Press.

Merriken v. Cressman, 364 F. Supp. 913 (E.D. Pa. 1973).

Meyer v. Nebraska, 262 U.S. 390 (1923).

Morris, R. A., Sales, B. D., & Berman, J. J. (1981). Research and the Freedom of Information Act. *American Psychologist, 36,* 819-826.

Mulvey, E. P., & Phelps, P. (1988). Ethical balances in juvenile justice research and practice. *American Psychologist, 43,* 65-69.

New Jersey v. T. L. O., 469 U.S. 325 (1985).

Olmstead v. United States, 277 U.S. 438 (1928).

Parham v. J. R., 442 U.S. 584 (1979).

Parke, R. D., & Sawin, D. B. (1979). Children's privacy in the home: Developmental, ecological, and child-rearing determinants. *Environment and Behavior, 11,* 84-104.

Pierce v. Society of Sisters, 268 U.S. 510 (1925).

Planned Parenthood of Central Missouri v. Danforth, 428 U.S. 52 (1976).

Prince v. Massachusetts, 321 U.S. 158 (1944).

Public Health Service (PHS) Act, as amended by the Health Omnibus Programs Extension of 1988, 42 U.S.C. § 242a.

Rivlin, L. G., & Wolfe, M. (1985). *Institutional settings in children's lives.* New York: John Wiley.

Roe v. Wade, 410 U.S. 113 (1973).

Rogers v. Okin, 634 F.2d 650 (1st Cir. 1980), *remanded on other grounds sub nom.* Mills vs. Rogers, 457 U.S. 291 (1982).

Roth, E. A., & Roth, L. H. (1984, April). *Children's feelings about psychiatric hospitalization: Legal and ethical implications.* Paper presented at the meeting of the American Orthopsychiatric Association, Toronto.

Schall v. Martin, 467 U.S. 253 (1984).

Small, M. A. (1988, March). *Factors in privacy expectations.* Paper presented at the meeting of the American Psychology-Law Society, Miami.

Small, M. A., & Wiener, R. L. (in press). Rethinking privacy torts: A view towards a psycholegal perspective. In D. K. Kagehiro & W. Laufer (Eds.), *Handbook of psychology and law.* New York: Springer Verlag.

Tremper, C. R. (1988). Respect for the human dignity of minors: What the Constitution requires. *Syracuse Law Review, 39,* 1293-1349.

Tremper, C. R., & Kelly, M. P. (1987). The mental health rationale for policies fostering minors' autonomy. *International Journal of Law and Psychiatry, 10,* 111-127.

United States v. Matlock, 415 U.S. 164 (1974).

Warren, S., & Brandeis, L. (1890). The right to privacy. *Harvard Law Review, 4,* 193-220.

Webster v. Reproductive Health Services, 109 S.Ct. 3040 (1989).

Wolfe, M. (1978). Childhood and privacy. In I. Altman & J. R. Wohlwill (Eds.), *Human behavior and environment: Advances in theory and research* (Vol. 3, pp. 175-222). New York: Plenum.

Yamamoto, K. (1979). Children's ratings of the stressfulness of experiences. *Developmental Psychology, 15,* 581-582.

5

Autonomy, Beneficence, and Child Development

An Ethical Analysis

RUTH MACKLIN

Introduction

Drawing on the other chapters in the volume, this chapter explores the concepts of autonomy and beneficence as they pertain to sensitive social and behavioral research with minors. Widely accepted ethical principles governing research are used to elucidate special features of sensitive research with such vulnerable groups as institutionalized minors, children who are in an oppositional relationship with their parents, and adolescents who are multiply stigmatized because of their drug use, homosexuality, delinquency, or HIV infection.

An attempt is made near the end of the chapter to ground such ethical concerns as autonomy and privacy in current theory and recent findings in developmental psychology. That effort is, at best, a tentative one, partly because of uncertainty about how the principle of autonomy can be related to changing developmental competencies as children mature, and partly because of the fact that self-theory in psychology is held to be "soft."

Despite the tentative aspect of that inquiry, the chief aim in the chapter is to pull together the various strands from theories of child development, applied research involving minors, pertinent laws and regulations, and the ethics of research on human subjects.

Does Social and Behavioral Research Pose Special Problems?

Ethical standards and legal regulations for research involving human subjects have been based largely on the biomedical model. Several different factors complicate the ethical picture concerning social and behavioral research. One factor is the variation in types of research that fall under this heading. Contrasts include observation versus intervention research; research on group behavior, including ethnographic studies (chapter 8), versus research with individuals; studies conducted by researchers working directly with subjects versus research mediated by agencies (chapters 6, 8, and 9). These different models suggest the possibility of different mechanisms for obtaining informed consent and different standards for preserving confidentiality. Would the establishment of different mechanisms or standards in these settings be ethically sound? Or would it be ethically dubious?

A second factor, which calls attention to the special features of sensitive research involving minors, is the existence and variation of community norms (chapter 9). Attitudes toward drug use and homosexuality vary among different groups in the population and in different regions of this country. So, too, do attitudes about adolescents' use of alcohol (chapter 9) and adolescent sexuality. Should community or regional norms be used as a standard for the acceptability of a proposed intervention? According to one viewpoint, these different social and cultural norms must be taken into account in the design of research protocols and in the mechanisms for obtaining consent. That view is open to the criticism that it subscribes to an unacceptable ethical relativism. Moreover, tailoring research protocols to varying social norms may impede the progress of social research because of conservative biases of segments of the population.

Additional complicating factors arise out of the research setting: when a research population is institutionalized, how does that affect the confidentiality of research data (chapter 6, 8, and 9), the consent procedures (chapter 6 and 8), and the voluntariness with which consent is granted by the subjects (chapter 6)? Ethical concerns dictate the need for special procedures and safeguards for research with adolescents who are institutionalized (chapter 6).

Obtaining Informed Consent

Parents are presumed to be the caretakers and decision makers for their minor children. Yet, parental authority over children is not absolute. In extreme situations, such as cases of abuse or neglect, children may be removed temporarily or even permanently from parental custody. In the biomedical context, parents normally are required to provide informed consent for treatment or research with their children. If parents refuse to consent to an established therapy likely to benefit their child, an attempt to override that refusal may be justified ethically and permitted legally. When a recommended therapy is still in the experimental stages, parents' refusal to grant consent is ethically permissible and would most likely not be overridden by a court order.

Despite years of thoughtful attention to the topic of informed consent for biomedical and behavioral treatment and research, some questions remain controversial or as yet unanswered. A number of these are especially pertinent to the issue of sensitive social and behavioral research with minors. One area of uncertainty continues to surround the concept of minors' *assent*: how, precisely, does it differ from *consent*? Assent is defined as "a child's affirmative agreement to participate in research." Moreover, "mere failure to object should not, absent affirmative agreement, be construed as assent" (45 C.F.R. 46.402). How much understanding is required for a child to properly give assent, and how might the notion of assent be relativized to the age and maturity of the child (chapter 7)?

A related set of questions pertains to the child's capacity to assent or consent (chapter 3, 4, and 7). How do the findings from research on child development bear on that capacity? From an ethical point of view, there may be as much cause for concern about children's ability to consent *voluntarily* as about their *understanding* of the purposes, risks, and benefits of the research.

Although parents are presumed to be the ones to consent for their children, the focus of this project has been to explore the circumstances that warrant a departure from this traditional presumption. Therefore, we need to ask and answer: Who may grant consent to research with minors *instead* of parents or legally authorized guardians? Is a school nurse ever an appropriate surrogate (chapter 8)? A superintendent or administrator of an institution (chapter 6)? A judge (chapter 9)? A court-appointed advocate? An important ethical distinction can be drawn between individuals who are *authorized* to consent on behalf of a minor, and those who truly represent the best interests of the child. No guarantee exists that a person who has been authorized to provide consent (perhaps but not necessarily in lieu of parental consent) will be a proper advocate for the minor.

Furthermore, *must* anyone be required to consent to certain types of research, in addition to parents or guardians: A school principal? The head of an agency (chapters 8 and 9)? A legislative body (chapter 8)? This last option invites contemplation on how removed from the interests of minors the consent procedures may become. Although legislative bodies allegedly represent "the people" in a democracy, it is undeniable that they are political bodies subject to pressures of special interest groups and powerful lobbies. Children have no political power, and vulnerable minors, such as gay youth, juvenile offenders, and adolescents at risk for acquiring HIV infection, are even more disenfranchised. Sufficient evidence exists of some politicians' insensitivity and lack of concern for groups such as gay men, intravenous drug users, and people with AIDS to warrant serious doubts about the appropriateness of having legislative bodies grant consent for sensitive social and behavioral research with minors.

Risk-Benefit Assessments

The risk-benefit ratio of a research protocol is a central criterion for evaluating its ethical acceptability. Behavioral and social research with minors requires risk-benefit assessments that differ from those typically found in biomedical research. In contrast to much biomedical research, social and behavioral studies typically do not promise much, if any, direct benefit to the research subjects (chapter 6). An exception lies in some types of intervention research (chapter 8), in which the dual aim is to alter high-risk patterns of adolescent behavior and to study how that might be achieved best.

Additionally, just as social and behavioral research typically does not offer much by way of direct benefit, neither is it likely to result in significant harm to subjects (chapter 3). Again, an exception can be found in AIDS research, where breach of confidentiality of HIV-related information can cause direct and significant social harm to research subjects (chapter 8). Another possible exception is that of research involving youth in juvenile detention centers, in which parents stand in nonbeneficent relationships with their children and in which custodial guardians in detention centers have interests that conflict with those of the minors in their custody (chapter 6).

The prospect of a favorable benefit-risk ratio and the need to obtain voluntary, informed consent from research subjects are separate and distinct ethical requirements. But when research with minors is of a sensitive nature, and when the subjects are mature minors, the risk-benefit ratio and the procedures for obtaining consent are linked closely. An ethical analysis is needed to determine whether the risk-benefit ratio of the research should affect the usual ethical requirements for parental consent and whether alternative mechanisms for obtaining consent are preferable.

Ethical Principles Governing Research

In *The Belmont Report* (NCPHS, 1979), the National Commission for the Protection of Human Subjects of Biomedical and Behavioral Research stated three principles, or general prescriptive judgments, relevant to research involving human subjects. The three principles are "Beneficence," "Justice," and "Respect for Persons." Drawn from long-established theories in philosophical ethics, these principles are now widely accepted as providing ethical standards for evaluating proposed research. Like any attempt to apply general principles in a specific situation, however, the application of these principles is not a simple or straightforward task. All three principles bear directly on the ethics of sensitive research involving minors.

Beneficence

Beneficence is understood as the obligation to maximize possible benefits and minimize possible harms (NCPHS, 1979, p. 4). This is simply another way of describing the obligation to obtain the most favorable benefit-risk ratio in designing and carrying out research. The commission paid particular attention to the application of this ethical principle to research involving children, because children are vulnerable and stand in greater need of protection than adult subjects of research. As the commission observed, "effective ways of treating childhood diseases and fostering healthy developments are benefits that serve to justify research involving children—even when individual research subjects are not direct beneficiaries" (NCPHS, 1979, p. 4). Because a large amount of social and behavioral research with children does not benefit the research subjects directly, the benefits to other children must outweigh any risks to the subjects themselves.

It is argued often that just as social and behavioral research typically does not benefit its subjects, neither is the risk of harm to subjects very great. If the standard model is that of invasive medical procedures conducted on pediatric patients, it may appear as if social and behavioral research poses only minimal risks. Nevertheless, the risks to research subjects are not limited to risks of physical harm; the concept of risk includes psychological and social risks, as well. When the research is investigating such sensitive subjects as minors' use of drugs or alcohol (chapter 9), when a breach of confidentiality might include disclosure of an adolescent's HIV infection (chapter 8), or when the research intrudes on a child's privacy (chapter 4), it is evident that psychological and social harm to minors can be considerable.

The *Belmont Report* refers to the "difficult ethical problem . . . about research that presents more than minimal risk without immediate prospect of direct benefit to the children involved" (NCPHS, 1979, pp. 4-5). Although it is probably true that most behavioral research does not fit this description (chapters 3 and 6), exceptions lie in such categories of sensitive research as minors' abuse of drugs or alcohol or other illegal activities.

An initial difficulty is how to define *minimal risk*. Federal regulations contain the following definition: "'Minimal risk' means that the risks of harm anticipated in the proposed research are not greater, considering probability and magnitude, than those ordinarily encountered in daily life or during the performance of routine physical or psychological examinations or tests" (45 C.F.R. 46.102[g]).

This definition gives rise to a second difficulty: should the risks of daily life be measured against a societal norm of risks children typically face in their everyday activities, or should those risks be measured against the actual background of minors who are the subjects of the research (chapter 3)? It is evident that these two standards may be widely disparate, especially in the case of sensitive research. If the minors are drug-using adolescents, those engaging in behaviors at high risk for acquiring HIV infection, juvenile offenders, or children who have been abused physically or sexually, the risks they encounter in their daily lives are of considerable magnitude. Thompson (chapter 3) argues that researchers should not necessarily define standards of minimal risk in terms of the ordinary life experiences of children in special populations such as "those who live in dangerous neighborhoods or have been maltreated or are substance abusers." Thompson's reason is that "by defining what is 'minimal risk' in terms of what is normative in the child's life experience, it potentially justifies researchers acting in ways that undermine the child even though these experiences may be familiar to the child."

Justice

A further elucidation of this objection requires a brief look at the second ethical principle noted in *The Belmont Report,* that of justice. To have anything other than a single standard for research on minors could lead to a violation of this ethical principle. One interpretation of the principle of justice is that "equals ought to be treated equally" (NCPHS, 1979, p. 5). But as the commission appropriately queried: "Who is equal and who is unequal? What considerations justify departure from equal distribution?" (NCPHS, 1979, p. 5). Without trying to answer that global question, we may venture a reply that pertains specifically to the question of what standard to use for determining "the risks of everyday life."

I propose that the standard of "minimal risk" be the same for all children and adolescents, *except* where the research being conducted is studying a particular social or behavioral area in which the everyday life of minors related to that activity places them at high risk of harm. Thus, research with minors who have been abused physically or sexually, research with adolescent crack or intravenous drug users, or research with sexually active youth at risk for acquiring HIV infection could be based on a higher level of risk of daily life than, say, biomedical research unrelated to the child's risky behavior or situation. In other words, "minimal risk" for minors conforms to a uniform, objective standard of calibrating risks of daily life except where the research focuses on the high-risk behavior or situation of the subjects.

This standard could permit research with minors that involves more than minimal risk yet provides no direct benefit to them, allowing for more than one standard of "minimal risk." To use different standards for research, depending on the specific characteristics of a subject population, is open to the critical charge of manipulating ethical standards to serve the needs of research. How can this be justified without violating the principle of justice?

The answer lies in seeing who will be the expected beneficiaries of this type of research. Because this group of minors is in a class of youth who are subject to high risks, anticipated benefits of the research will accrue to this same group. *The Belmont Report* states: "Justice demands that . . . research should not unduly involve persons from groups unlikely to be among the beneficiaries of subsequent applications" (NCPHS, 1979, p. 5). Conversely, if the only way to provide benefit to members of these groups is to conduct research involving those groups, a higher level of risk may be justified by the prospect of future benefits. Thus, the use of different standards of "minimal risk," geared to specific subject populations, does not violate the principle of justice in research, but rather comports with that principle.

Respect for Persons

Because children are vulnerable, and especially because research might not provide direct benefit to them, the issue of consent to their participation becomes paramount. When adults are subjects of research, they are presumed capable of providing consent on their own behalf. The respect-for-persons principle, which holds that "individuals should be treated as autonomous agents" (NCPHS, 1979, p. 4), is geared to the requirement of informed consent. A fuller picture of the basis of this ethical requirement is spelled out in *The Belmont Report*:

> An autonomous person is an individual capable of deliberation about personal goals and of acting under the direction of such deliberation. To respect autonomy is to give weight to autonomous persons' considered opinions and choices while refraining from obstructing their actions unless they are clearly detrimental to others. (p. 4)

Is an adolescent an autonomous person? At what age does a child become autonomous, in the sense depicted here? The commission was silent on this matter. The respect-for-persons principle is intended to apply only to adults. Yet the principle incorporates a second important ethical conviction: "Persons with diminished autonomy are entitled to protection" (p. 4). This second ethical conviction is described more fully as follows:

... [N]ot every human being is capable of self-determination. The capacity for self-determination matures during an individual's life and some individuals lose this capacity wholly or in part because of illness, mental disability, or circumstances that severely restrict liberty. Respect for the immature and the incapacitated may require protecting them as they mature or while they are incapacitated." (p. 4)

The two ethical principles—beneficence and respect for persons—are usually construed as separate and coequal principles to guide the conduct of biomedical and behavioral research. Yet they are linked in a number of critical respects when applied to sensitive research with minors. The first respect to consider is that of waivers of parental consent.

Several factors relate to waivers of parental consent:

1. The risks to children of disclosing information to their parents, as part of the consent process. One viewpoint holds that the higher the risks of disclosure, the more a waiver is ethically appropriate.

2. Benefits to children from being part of certain intervention research programs, such as potentially high-gain intervention research on risk factors for AIDS (chapter 8). As in factor 1, a presumption favoring waiver of parental consent may exist when the potential benefit to the minor is high. Factors 1 and 2 might be combined, resulting in a more refined analysis.

3. The maturity of the minor. According to one view, the fact that a minor is "mature," taken by itself, does not render parental consent unreasonable (chapter 6). It may well be, however, that if the research stands to provide considerable benefit to the minor, such as an AIDS intervention program, or if involving the parent in the consent process stands to harm the interests of the minor, then the maturity of the minor becomes a significant factor in a determination to waive parental consent. Maturity becomes significant because mature minors can be assumed to have greater capacity for judgment and, therefore, an increased ability to weigh the risks and benefits of participating based on their own values. It would be necessary then to determine when the maturity of the minor should be factored in—at an initial stage of deciding whether a waiver of parental consent is justified, or only after the risks and benefits to the subjects have been calculated.

4. It must be kept in mind that an alternative to waiving parental consent is to forgo the research program entirely. Although this option is likely to

be unpopular with social and behavioral researchers, it requires an objective assessment of the importance of the research as a contribution to knowledge, as well as a prediction of its practical value for delivering beneficial services to needy groups of adolescents. As with any risk-benefit assessment, the cost of *not* doing the research must be factored into the analysis.

Developmental Psychology, Autonomy, and Privacy

Autonomy is the result of cognitive and emotional processes that mature as individuals approach adulthood. Consequently, knowledge about child development might be useful in developing ethical standards for research involving minors. Paternalistic behavior toward infants and young children is justified ethically; indeed, it is ethically obligatory. But because the capacity for self-determination matures during an individual's life, at some point paternalism exercised by parents, teachers, and other authorities must give way to respect for the minor's autonomy.

The literature in child development may help provide answers to the question: When can minors be considered sufficiently mature to consent on their own behalf? For most purposes, that question is answered simply and arbitrarily by drawing a sharp line at a chronological age—typically, 18—at which the age of majority begins. The focus of the present study forces us to consider alternative standards to that of chronological age.

The language of statutes and judicial opinions has been couched in terms of the *mature minor,* whereas the language of ethics employs the concept of *autonomy.* Both concepts deserve a closer look.

"Mature" Minor

Three leading candidates compete for how to define *mature minor:* (a) contextually, by reference to working, living, or marital status that would apply to all minors having that status; (b) functionally, drawing on findings in cognitive/developmental psychology; and (c) individually, making a case-by-case assessment.

The contextual method looks simply at what the minor's status is, such as "emancipated: living, working, and perhaps raising families independent of their parents" (chapter 6). Another example is found in an Illinois statute "that provides that a minor 16 years of age or over who has demonstrated the capacity to manage his own affairs may be partially or completely emancipated."

A functional method could ignore status or context and look instead at adolescents' general cognitive and social developmental characteristics, such as the finding that "minors older than 13 may have decision-making capacities similar to those of most adults, at least for purposes of some kinds of research or treatment decisions" (chapter 6). This approach would look at stages of development, seeking to draw a rough age-based line informed by psychological research (chapters 3 and 7).

The third method, making case-by-case assessments, would be a blend of the other approaches yet would require that the maturity of each child be evaluated individually for the purpose at hand. This approach is illustrated in the Supreme Court's decision in *Bellotti v. Baird* (1979), which entitles "mature" minors to obtain abortions without the knowledge or permission of their parents. The Court set forth a three-part criterion: first, the determination of maturity must be made on a case-by-case basis; second, a mature minor need not be economically independent of her parents; and third, the minor should be "mature enough and well enough informed to make an abortion decision" (*Bellotti v. Baird*, 1979). This ruling does not amount to a definition of *mature minor* but is, rather, a requirement that determinations of maturity in regard to abortion decisions must be made on a case-by-case basis.

Autonomy

At first glance, the concept of autonomy turns out to be no clearer than that of "mature minor." Autonomy is confused sometimes with freedom or liberty to act. When used in this way, as a synonym for *self-determination*, autonomy is a thin concept. It presupposes only that behavior is voluntary and intentional (Miller, 1981). The behavior of even very young children can satisfy this minimal definition of autonomy. A richer notion is suggested by the etymology of the word, which literally means "self-rule." Autonomy in this sense has its roots in the moral philosophy of Immanuel Kant (1785/1959), who held that a necessary condition for morality is possession of a "self-legislating will."

Self-rule requires two basic ingredients: first, an authentic, well-developed self; and second, an independent capacity to rule the self.

These ingredients are captured in a formula proposed by the philosopher Gerald Dworkin: "autonomy = authenticity + independence" (Dworkin, 1976). This formula contains the beginnings of a full-bodied concept of autonomy, richer than simply the freedom to act. Research data in developmental psychology can enhance our understanding of the growth and nature of the self from the time of earliest infancy, when babies are unable to distinguish themselves from the rest of their world, through the time of maturity when fully autonomous and responsible behavior may occur.

The development of a concept of the self, formal operational thought, critical self-evaluation, and the ability to make appropriate use of self-conscious emotional reactions (shame, guilt, embarrassment, and pride) have been reported in the psychological literature (see chapter 3). These processes of psychological development described by Thompson (chapter 3) are equally applicable to understanding the development of autonomy. The growth of a self-concept embodies a capacity for abstract thought, along with growing cognitive skills. These capacities are necessary but not sufficient for a full-bodied concept of autonomy.

One sense of autonomy that focuses on these cognitive elements has been termed "autonomy as effective deliberation. . . . This means action taken where a person believed that he or she was in a situation calling for a decision, was aware of the alternatives and the consequences of the alternatives, evaluated both, and chose an action based on that evaluation" (Miller, 1981, p. 24). This sense of autonomy overlaps with that of rational capacity, developing as children make the transition to formal-operational thought (chapter 3).

If autonomy is understood as comprising both a well-developed self-concept and a capacity for self-rule, then the ability of minors to grant voluntary, informed consent to research requires more than the acquisition of cognitive skills. "Autonomy as effective deliberation" needs to be supplemented by additional concepts, such as a sense of self-esteem and the capacity for critical self-evaluation (chapter 3).

Harms, Wrongs, and Rights

One reason for the central importance of autonomy for ethics is its link with the concept of *rights*. It is precisely these rights for which the "respect for persons" principle mandates respect. Individuals not only have a right not to be harmed, physically and psychologically, they also have a right not to suffer *wrongs* at the hands of others. One way of wronging people—even though they may not be harmed directly—is by deceiving them.

Thompson shows how young children may be harmed in research maneuvers that involve manipulations and deception: "Young children's understanding of authority renders them more vulnerable to coercive manipulations than older children. . . . Furthermore, young children's trust of authorities makes them more vulnerable to being deceived in research." This greater vulnerability on the part of younger children makes them more susceptible to being harmed as research subjects. Yet despite older children's increased immunity from this species of harm, by virtue of their growing autonomy older children are at risk of being wronged, as well as harmed, by deception.

For all children, an additional danger exists. When children serving as research subjects are wronged in a way that is obvious to them, it can pose a problem for their perception of authority figures. Children are still in the rudimentary stages of forming beliefs about who is permitted to do what in society. If a physician, psychologist, or scientist behaves toward the child in a way the child has already learned is wrong, it could give the child the idea that important people or those in authority may act in ways prohibited to others.

It is held sometimes that "debriefing" can eliminate ethical problems surrounding deception in research. Debriefing following a deceptive research maneuver, however, cannot constitute a retrospective righting of the wrong. Moreover, it may inflict an additional harm by damaging the subject's self-esteem. In the case of minors, especially young children, debriefing can be most harmful when it reveals the wrong or when it conveys information that will confuse the child further.

An example of the latter situation could occur in research on moral development, in which money is left lying around to see what factors will affect whether the young child picks up the money. It has been argued that children who lack a clear concept of stealing should not be debriefed. Four-year-olds know little about the concept of stealing except that it is something very bad people do; yet 4-year-olds themselves steal without realizing that they are stealing. Picking up the money in the research situation is something most 4-year-olds would do. The dilemma lies in wanting neither to support nor blame the child for picking up the money.[1]

The issue of debriefing children who are subjects in social and behavioral research is addressed in the American Psychological Association's

(APA, 1982) publication, *Ethical Principles in the Conduct of Research with Human Participants.* The book states:

> With children, the primary objective of the postinvestigation clarification procedure is to ensure that the child leaves the research situation with no undesirable aftereffects of participation. Attaining this objective may mean, for example, that certain misconceptions should not be removed or even that some new misconceptions should be induced. If children erroneously believe that they have done well on a research task, there may be more harm in trying to correct this misconception than in permitting it to remain. Conversely, ameliorative efforts are needed when children feel that they have done poorly. In some circumstances, such efforts may include using special experimental procedures to guarantee the child a final experience of success. (pp. 65-66)

In endorsing this approach, the APA quite clearly uses a consequentialist moral principle to determine what is the ethically correct practice. In striving to ensure that children are not harmed by psychological research, the profession permits them to be wronged by suggesting that "new misconceptions should be induced" in certain circumstances. Probing questions must be raised about whether the contributions to human knowledge are so important that they require deliberate lying to children and manipulating them in the ways suggested by the APA "ethical" principle just cited.

Other critically important ethical concerns in sensitive social and behavioral research with minors are privacy and confidentiality. Children may suffer harm to their interests when their privacy is invaded or when their confidentiality as research subjects is breached (chapters 3 and 4). But in addition to being *harmed,* children—like adults—may be *wronged* by such intrusions (chapter 4). If minors have a moral right to privacy, then it is a violation of that right for another to intrude. The determination of when to ascribe the right to privacy to minors should rest on findings in developmental psychology.

Research has shown the importance of privacy to children. In chapter 4, Melton sketches the psychological basis and the legal doctrine of privacy as it pertains to children. We are confronted with the ethical problem of determining when children should be considered to have *moral* rights to privacy against their parents. Posing that question is another way of inquiring into the autonomy of minors: When do they deserve to be respected as persons, regarding their right to privacy? A closely related question is: When may or should information about minors be kept confidential, even (or, perhaps, especially) from their parents?

One of the best illustrations of the relationship between developmental psychology and the moral concept of autonomy lies in the increasing right to privacy as the child matures. With increasing age, privacy becomes increasingly important as a marker of independence and self-esteem (chapter 3). Research reveals that the first concept of privacy to emerge in children is "territorial privacy," followed at a later age by a concern for "informational privacy" (chapters 3 and 4). The latter notion is of crucial importance in the research setting, posing the question of when a "right to privacy" properly emerges.

An anecdote drawn from a personal (nonresearch) experience illustrates the uncertainty surrounding a child's right to privacy and the question of legitimate parental authority to invade the child's realm. I was visiting a friend with a child who was about 6 years old. The child's bedroom was on the second floor of the home. When he was younger, his mother had installed a speaker system so she could hear him cry or call for her when she was downstairs. Now at age 6, the child slept in a regular bed, had a night-light in his room, would go to the bathroom by himself, and otherwise tend to his needs. After he had gone to bed upstairs, his mother and I were downstairs in the kitchen and the speaker system was turned on. The child was talking to himself and to his toy animals, and I had the distinct sense of eavesdropping on his conversation. I asked his mother whether she thought at this age, we might be invading his privacy. She responded at first with surprise, the idea never having occurred to her. Then with denial: "He's still a little boy, and the speaker's been in his room since he was a baby. He's used to it. Besides, what if he needs me?"

No doubt, a sharp line cannot demarcate the emergence of a right to privacy. Uncertainty may exist regarding a 6-year-old child's right to territorial or informational privacy. But by age 10 that right probably deserves considerable respect, and to eavesdrop on the conversation of teenagers is an unequivocal violation of their rights. The emergence of privacy rights in a child serves as an example of how the development of autonomy in minors must give rise to a corresponding diminution of parental rights of control.

In sensitive research with minors, questions of privacy and confidentiality cannot be separated from those of beneficence. If a potential for harm befalling minor subjects exists when information is disclosed to parents about drug abuse, sexual behavior, or a risk of HIV infection, it may require researchers to provide strict protections for the minors' confidentiality. If releasing information to parents would alter significantly the risk-benefit ratio of the research, some research that might be acceptable under strict confidentiality protections would become unacceptable if disclosure were practiced.

An opposing view would argue that parents have a *right* to such information. Like any claim about rights, this claim gives rise to a question about how the right is to be derived. Providing a sound derivation for rights claims has been a thorny problem for moral philosophers, but all are agreed on at least one point. People's mere desires or preferences—however strong they may be—do not constitute a sufficient basis for claiming that a right exists. It follows that a parental "right" to information about their children cannot be derived simply from what parents themselves desire or what they believe they are entitled. Similarly, custom and tradition do not provide a satisfactory ethical justification for claims about parental rights, regardless of how well entrenched those customs may be.

Another point for further study is the relationship between the requirement of parental consent for social and behavioral research with children and the need to disclose to parents information obtained in the research. These two questions might have different answers. Circumstances may exist in which parental consent to their children's participation in social or behavioral research is ethically necessary, yet where information learned in the research should nonetheless be kept from them. Conversely, circumstances may exist in which a waiver of parental consent is justified but where information learned in the course of research should be disclosed. An example might be the discovery of HIV infection in an adolescent, resulting from a study conducted in a drug treatment program in which the minor was enrolled. Disclosure might be necessary in order to obtain medical treatment or early intervention to combat the HIV infection, for which parental knowledge and consent would be ethically appropriate and legally required.

What is needed to help resolve these quandaries is a background moral theory of the parent-child relationship, addressing the changes in this relationship as the child grows older. This theory would include an account of the grounds for assigning rights and duties, responsibilities, and obligations. Against a background theory of this sort, a parental "need to know" would exist in some but not all instances, and parental rights might be derivable from those needs.

Although I am unaware of any fully developed theory of the parent-child relationship, several authors have illuminated a number of key ingredients.[2] Peter G. Brown (1982) sketches an account of parental responsibility that can serve as a standard against which to measure the moral authority of the parent to give or withhold proxy consent on behalf of his or her child. Taking a traditional stance, Margaret O'Brien Steinfels argues that "parental authority is necessary . . . for the provision of the child's physical, social, and emotional well-being and the protection of the child's interests" (Steinfels, 1982, p. 245). Although these accounts are helpful in articulating some general features of a moral relationship, they do not address the central concerns that involve adolescents, their parents, and sensitive social and behavioral research.

Conclusion

As the chapters in this volume demonstrate, well-confirmed psychological theories and reliable empirical data from the social and behavioral sciences provide a strong foundation for an inquiry into sensitive research involving minors. To that foundation must be added the ethical principles necessary for being able to draw any conclusions about what ought to be done in this area. Even when the psychological theories and empirical data are well founded, and even if the ethical principles themselves are accepted widely, reasonable people may still disagree about particular issues regarding parental consent, confidentiality, and the assessment of risk-benefit ratios.

Discovering where such disagreements lie is the first step in seeking to resolve them. When biomedical and behavioral research involves children and adolescents, an even greater need exists for ethical vigilance than when the subjects of research are autonomous adults. A thorough ethical analysis, informed by a variety of viewpoints, is a prelude to the future task of proposing changes in existing policies and practices.

Notes

1. I owe this example and the preceding discussion to the helpful comments of Joan Sieber.

2. See, for example, the essays in the volume *Having Children* (O'Neill & Ruddick, 1989), especially Jeffrey Bluestein, "Child Rearing and Family Interests" (pp. 115-122).

References

American Psychological Association. (1982). *Ethical principles in the conduct of research with human participants.* Washington, DC.

Bellotti v. Baird 443 U.S. 622 (1979).

Bluestein, J. (1989). Child rearing and family interests. In O. O'Neill & W. Ruddick (Eds.), *Having children* (pp. 115-122). New York: Oxford University Press.

Brown, P. G. (1982). Human independence and parental proxy consent. In W. Gaylin & R. Macklin (Eds.), *Who speaks for the child: The problems of proxy consent* (pp. 209-222). New York: Plenum.

Dworkin, G. (1976). Autonomy and behavior control. *Hastings Center Report, 6,* 23-28.

45 C.F.R. 46.102(g).

45 C.F.R. 46.402.

Kant, I. (1959). *Foundations of the metaphysics of morals.* New York: Macmillan. (Original work published 1785)

Miller, B. (1981). Autonomy and the refusal of lifesaving treatment. *Hastings Center Report, 11,* 22-28.

National Commission for the Protection of Human Subjects of Biomedical and Behavioral Research (NCPHS). (1979). *The Belmont report.* Washington, DC: Department of Health, Education, and Welfare.

O'Neill, O., & Ruddick, W. (Eds.). (1989). *Having children.* New York: Oxford University Press.

Steinfels, M. O. (1982). Children's rights, parental rights, family privacy, and family autonomy. In W. Gaylin & R. Macklin (Eds.), *Who speaks for the child: The problems of proxy consent* (pp. 223-263). New York: Plenum.

PART II

The Consent Process

6

Minors' Assent to Behavioral Research Without Parental Consent

THOMAS GRISSO

Federal regulations for research with minors (Department of Health and Human Services, 1983/1988) explicitly recognize that minors are entitled to exercise an influence on decisions about their research participation, independent of their parents' decisions.

According to regulations before the 1980s, a minor's research participation often simply required the parent's informed consent. In essence, the minor was volunteered by the parent. Current regulations, however, require more. Parents still must be informed adequately, and they still must be asked to decide whether to allow their child's participation in research. The relevant regulation, 46.408 (b), however, does not construe their decision as "consent." That is, their decision is not a condition that clears the way for research participation of the child. Instead, the regulation establishes the parents' role as that of deciding to "permit" or "deny" their child's participation. "Denial" blocks the child's participation. But "permission," unlike "consent," does not automatically allow the child's participation, because 46.408 (a) of the DHHS regulations gives the minor the role of deciding to "assent" or "refuse." The minor's research participation, therefore, ordinarily can occur only in the combination of parental permission plus child assent. Either a parent's denial of permission or a child's refusal negates the child's participation.

As Melton (1988) has noted, this approach appears to be unique in law. It promotes shared decision making and, in essence, provides independent veto power by parent and minor in matters concerning the minor's research participation.

This arrangement seeks a balance in providing adequate protection in two respects. Were the decision solely that of the minor, often we would be concerned about whether the minor understood the research procedures to which he or she was making a commitment. We also might question the minor's capacity to make a voluntary assent that is more than merely acquiescent. Concerns about involuntary assent may be raised because of the minor's developmental level or the disparity between the minor's social status and that of the adult researcher whom the minor may perceive as having the ultimate control and power in the situation.

In contrast, were the decision solely that of the parent, ordinarily we would be more assured about matters of understanding that to which consent is being given and about the parent's ability to make a voluntary, nonpressured consent or refusal. On the other hand, a parent-only decision places the minor—whose participation is being requested—in the role of one who is "lent out" to the researcher, so to speak, ignoring the fact that the minor is a person who may have his or her own reasons for not wishing to undergo a research procedure.

For most social science and behavioral research, which ordinarily involves no direct benefit to the minor, the principle of equal veto by parent and child would not seem particularly controversial. This is not to say that it will never raise conflicts. For example, imagine a situation in which a particular child may be reluctant to assent to a harmless research procedure because it causes the child to have to forfeit a desired play activity. The parent, in turn, believes that the child should participate in order to learn the altruistic values of contributing to the welfare of others by volunteering. Arguably, the parent has the child's best interest at heart, as well as a responsibility to train the child in such values. The new regulations do raise this sort of conflict.

On balance, however, the principle of equal veto by parents and children under 46.408 (a) and (b) is less potentially controversial than the provisions of 46.408 (c). This section of the regulations allows minors' participation in research, in certain cases, to occur without the parents' or guardian's involvement and on the decision of the child alone.

This chapter focuses primarily on the provisions for waiver of parental/guardian involvement in the decision under 46.408 (c) and avoids extensive discussion of the provision in 46.408 (a) concerning waiver of the requirement for minors' assent. It is worthwhile to explain briefly why the provisions in Paragraph *a* will receive less attention here.

The provisions that allow by-pass of children's decision making (46.408 [a]) focus on two types of circumstances. First, they allow waiver of the minor's assent in research that is very important for the health or well-being of the child. But my focus here is on behavioral and social science research, which rarely involves studies that offer any substantial direct benefit to the actual participants. So it will be rare in behavioral research to waive the minor's role in the decision on the basis of the direct benefit of the research.

Second, they allow waiver of the minor's assent when, according to 46.408 (a), "they cannot reasonably be consulted." I believe that for participation in nonemergency, nonmedical, behavioral and social science research, the term *reasonable* may be interpreted quite liberally. Note that the question here is not whether the minor can provide informed consent, but whether the minor can be "consulted." In other words, can the minor be made to understand what will happen in the research study and why the study is being done? Reviews of relevant developmental research (e.g., Weithorn, 1983) indicate that most children can be consulted one way or another, as long as the researchers speak their language. The notable exceptions might be children who are moderately or more severely retarded in intellectual capacities and those with certain serious and disabling forms of child psychopathology.

Therefore, when referring to behavioral science research that does not offer direct benefit to the minor, the provisions of 46.408 (a) for by-passing the minor's assent will not often be invoked. It is more likely to be relevant in those minority of behavioral research studies that offer some treatment benefit.

In contrast, 46.408 (c), dealing with waiver of parents' and guardians' decision making about their child's participation, may be invoked with relatively greater frequency in a wide range of behavioral and social science research studies; therefore, it offers greater challenges in interpretation.

Exploration of its implications requires addressing two broad questions. First, *when* might Paragraph *c* apply? In what kinds of circumstances might one argue for proceeding with minors' assent or refusal as the deciding factor without involving parents or guardians in the decision?

Second, if 46.408 (c) is applied, then *how* should this be done? What additional protections might be needed when parents' or guardians' permission is waived as a requirement?

Elements of 45 CFR 46.408 (c)

First, let us look more closely at the wording of 46.408 (c). It is somewhat awkwardly constructed as an "If-then-if-if" statement. That is, "If faced with condition A, then you may do B, but only if you also do C, and if condition D also exists." The following uses quotations from portions of the text of 46.408 (c) but is not a complete quotation; it is an adaptation intended to convey the meaning of the text in clearer and more structured form:

> *If:* "the IRB determines that a research protocol is designed for conditions or for a subject population for which parental or guardian permission is not a reasonable requirement to protect the subjects (for example, neglected or abused children)";
>
> *then:* "it may waive" the DHHS requirements for informed consent and parental permission;
>
> *if:* "an appropriate mechanism for protecting the children who will participate as subjects in the research is substituted;" and
>
> *if:* "waiver is not inconsistent with federal, state or local law."

One might add that by implication this provision still requires the minors' assent, as long as the minors involved are capable of being consulted.

Apart from the rule that waiver of parental permission must be legally allowable, two of the phrases are critical. The first phrase refers to waiver of parents' permission if it *is not a reasonable requirement to protect the subjects.*

As noted earlier, the need for protection is raised by two dangers. That is, researchers want to make sure that minors know and appreciate that to which they may be assenting; and researchers want to be sure that if minors assent, it is not merely an acquiescent response to the adult researcher's request. Ordinarily, the parent could assist the minor to understand the procedures and to make a voluntary decision.

What Paragraph *c* refers to, therefore, is situations in which parents' or guardians' involvement would *not* constitute protection from these two dangers, thus causing their involvement not to be a reasonable requirement.

What conditions or subject populations are likely to be involved? What types of research situations, types of parents or guardians, and types of minor subjects raise the possibility for waiving parental permission? I will look at that in a moment.

The second phrase requires the substitution of *an appropriate mechanism for protecting the children who will participate.* If parent or guardian involvement is to be waived, how can researchers mitigate their concern about the possibility of inadequate understanding and acquiescent assent by minors acting independently?

The DHHS regulation itself does not give much guidance for determining the specific meaning of either of these questions. Accompanying the phrase "not a reasonable requirement" is the brief reference to neglected or abused children. But since this reference is offered only as an example, one can presume that the provision was not intended to be applied exclusively to situations of neglected children. Other situations also may be included, but the regulation does not provide the principle that would be needed to guide IRBs' and researchers' discretion.

Concerning the term "appropriate substituted mechanisms," parts of Paragraph *c* that were not provided in the above quotation go on to list factors that should be considered when deciding on a substituted mechanism. Those listed are the nature and purpose of the research, risks and benefits to the subjects, and the subjects' age, maturity, status, and condition. Yet the regulation does not show, by example or principle, what role these factors should play in guiding IRBs' or researchers' discretion.

One place to start in fleshing out these two elements of the regulations is the recommendations of the National Commission for the Protection of Human Subjects in Biomedical and Behavioral Research (1977). The regulations themselves were written in language that was almost identical to the commission's recommendation. That recommendation was accompanied by commentary that provided more examples and some reasoning for the recommended provision for waiver of parental permission. The following discussion attempts to put more structure on the examples used in the commentary so that they might provide some conceptual guidelines for applying 46.408 (c).

As noted earlier, the discussion will focus on behavioral research that offers little or no direct benefit to the research participant because these conditions characterize most behavioral and social science research.

"Not a Reasonable Requirement to Protect the Subjects"

What was intended by the phrase "not a reasonable requirement to protect"? In what situations might parental permission not be a reasonable requirement to protect children who might participate in proposed social science and behavioral research? After I have considered several possible conditions, I then will return to the question of substituted mechanisms for dealing with those conditions.

Four types of situations might be relevant for waiving the requirement for parental or guardian permission:

1. The parents are *incompetent.*
2. The parents are competent, but *unavailable.*
3. The parents are competent and available but *in a nonbeneficent posture.*
4. The parents are competent, available, and beneficent, but their participation is *superfluous.*

Incompetence. The matter of parents' incompetence, the first of the situations above, was raised as an example in the commission's commentary of one instance in which parents' permission might be waived. The reasoning, presumably, is that if parents have serious decision-making incapacities—for example, because of serious mental retardation or mental illness—then they might not provide the protection against poor understanding and against acquiescent assent that the parental permission requirement was intended to provide.

When applied to questions of minors' participation in social science and behavioral research, however, one may argue that Paragraph *c* rarely would need to be invoked solely because of parent incompetence.

Many minors whose parents are functionally and legally incompetent are already under the guardianship of someone other than, or in addition to, their parents (a relative, foster parent, guardian ad litem, or agency): someone who is authorized to make decisions about the minor that otherwise would be made by the parent. As long as such competent guardians exist, Paragraph *c* need not be invoked merely because of parental incompetence, because the 46.408 (b) requirement to obtain parental permission refers to "parent *or* guardian," and in many cases the authorized guardian will take the role.

But what if there are no guardians? For example, imagine that a researcher wishes to perform a psychological study involving trainable mentally retarded youths. The proposed research sample includes students of a day school, but the students all live at home with their parents, whose behaviors have not presented evidence of neglect sufficient to raise questions of their legal incompetence. Empirical correlations between parent and child regarding intellectual capacity and adaptive functioning suggest that the parents as a group may be expected to have very limited intellectual capacities. They might have sufficient capacities to meet everyday needs of the child, but not sufficient for understanding the implications of the particular research proposal itself.

Thus, in some situations both parent and child, in the absence of any available guardian, are poorly prepared to protect against poor understanding and acquiescent assent. In these circumstances, it may be necessary to develop appropriate substitute mechanisms to ensure these protections. But do the parents' questionable functional incapacities provide a reason for waiving parents' permission, as the commission suggested?

One may argue that it does not and that such parents ordinarily should be consulted despite their incapacities. The logic of this argument may be the same as the commission's in deciding that minors themselves should be consulted and have independent veto power. In that logic, minors' possible incapacities to understand and to make voluntary assent was not seen as a reason to exclude them from the decision about participation; they were seen as having an independent interest that should be honored, but that ordinarily parents would have to provide the additional protection. Similarly, *parents* with intellectual deficiencies also have an independent interest in their children that should be honored, although further steps might need to be taken to ensure the protection that parents ordinarily are expected to afford.

In summary, contrary to the commission's suggestion, it is difficult to imagine situations in which the incompetence or intellectual deficiencies of parents would constitute a reason to waive the requirement for parental or guardian permission under 46.408 (c), at least for most social science and behavioral research proposals. In cases of a formal declaration of incompetence of the parent, society usually will have authorized a guardian who can provide the required permission. In cases of no formal guardian or declaration of parental incompetence, one may argue persuasively that parents have an independent interest that should be included in the decision about their child's research participation. Their incapacities suggest the need for additional protections for the child, which I will discuss later, but need not include a by-pass of the parents' role in the decision altogether.

Unavailability. The second situation is the unavailability of parent or guardian. This circumstance may come into play when parental or guardian participation would be impractical or impossible to obtain and when the research itself is potentially very important for society and cannot be performed without minors' participation.

The commission offered one example. It made note that the laws of many states allow minors' access to medical treatment for certain purposes without parental consent: for example, treatment for venereal disease, alcoholism, and, in some states, abortion. These laws recognize that if minors were required to seek their parents' permission for treatment of these types, some minors might not receive the benefit of adequate and necessary treatment because they would be reluctant to make their parents aware of their conditions.

The commission reasoned that research designed to determine factors related to these specific medical conditions and treatments also could be performed without parental permission. The commission's logic on this matter was influenced by the fact that important research on these conditions simply could not be done if parental permission were required. Note that the laws mentioned above focus on waiver of parental permission *in order to assure treatment benefits* to the minor, whereas the commission focused on waiver in order to *allow important research to be accomplished* when requiring parental permission would prohibit the research.

The law and the commission's example deal with research in medical procedures. Many *nonmedical* research situations exist in which parents are, in effect, unavailable to the researcher. That is, the minor controls the researcher's access to the parents, and the minor will participate only while denying that access. Thus, the parent is unavailable, and the research cannot proceed if parental permission is required.

For example, imagine a researcher who wishes to study the psychological status of minors who have run away from home and who are temporarily living in runaway meccas with similarly situated minors. Often, they may not be willing to reveal their parents' identities or locations or would refuse to participate if their participation required such revelation. For a second example, imagine a researcher who has gained the confidence of some neighborhood delinquent gang members who are willing to participate in confidential research interviews about their motivations for becoming involved and the rewards of their activities. They will refuse to do it, however, if their parents must be contacted, because many of them do not want their parents to know about their gang associations.

These examples manifest unavailability of parents as a consequence of minors' control of access to them. Other types of unavailability might arise, however, even if parents are identifiable, are in proximity to the researcher, and the minors themselves would raise no objection to their involvement.

My students and I encountered a situation of this type in a research study we performed in the 1970s (Grisso, 1981). It involved 12- to 17-year-old minors in a juvenile court detention center after their arrests on delinquency charges. The study required administration of a few research measures and interviews to 400 participants within 3 days after their admission to detention. The conditions for valid results would have been violated if the procedure were delayed beyond that time period.

At the time the written research proposal for this study was prepared, we fully expected to seek parents' permission when they first visited their child in detention. State law required that police notify parents immediately upon their child's arrest and that detention personnel request the parents' presence within 24 hours of admission to detention.

To test our ability to get parents' permission, we stationed research assistants at the detention intake on a 24-hour basis for 7 consecutive days. We wanted to find out what percentage of parents showed up, for the population of boys who eventually remained in detention beyond 18 hours and therefore would be candidates for research participation. To our dismay, we found that only 13% of that population received visits from parents at any time in the first 3 days of their detention.

We had already been notified that we were going to receive federal funding for this study, and panic set in. One alternative, we reasoned, might be to telephone or drive to the parents' homes to seek their consent in the first 24 hours of the child's detention. But the juvenile court would not approve this plan, and for good reason: During that same 24 hours, the court's juvenile officers often drove to parents' homes to try to persuade them to agree to take their child *out* of detention!

Had 46.408 (c) been available to us then, its provisions might have offered an option. But that DHHS regulation was not then in effect. One might think that the dilemma could be solved on the basis of guardianship. That is, the juvenile court itself was, in effect, the temporary guardian of the juveniles while they were in its custody, and many states' laws authorize the court to use wide discretion in making decisions about its wards that normally would be reserved for parental discretion. The matter, however, was not that simple, as you will see in the discussion of the next question.

In summary, the unavailability of parents, coupled with a pressing social need for certain types of behavioral research, provides one situation in which parental permission may not be a reasonable requirement and for which one might consider the application of 46.408 (c) for waiver of parental permission.

Nonbeneficence. A third type of situation occurs when circumstances cast the parent or recognized guardian in a potentially nonbeneficent or adversarial stance in relation to the child. The parent might be both competent and available, but circumstances are such that the parent's participation simply would not provide the protection it is meant to provide, because of breakdown in the usual parent-child relationship.

The commission's example that best fits this type of circumstance involves children who have been neglected or abused by their parents or whose parents have turned them over to juvenile court or child welfare agents for allegedly being incorrigible.

At least two things are implied by such situations. One is that by the parents' acts, one can no longer make the usual assumption that the parents will act beneficently to protect the child's interest when deciding about permission. Thus, the parents' decision about such matters is no longer a reasonable (that is, a rational) requirement for the child's protection. For example, parents who have abused their children might be motivated by personal or self-protective interests to veto their children's participation in research designed to understand and meet the needs of neglected or abused children themselves.

In other instances, parents in nonbeneficent relationships with their children might have a coercive influence on the child, thus rendering the child's own assent involuntary. This problem was raised, for example, in the juvenile detention center described previously, in which an attempt was made to obtain parents' permission in the few instances in which the parents did show up soon after their child's arrest. After parents had arrived at the detention center and finished responding to police inquiries, my students and I tried taking them aside with their child and attempting to engage them in the research permission process. Often this attempt proved to be meaningless. Faced with their child's recent arrest, some parents were frightened and could not decide anything. Others were depressed, and still others were very angry at their child. One parent responded, "You want to test him? You want to hold him here a few days and make him take a bunch of tests? Sure, why not? Serves him right!" Then, turning angrily to the boy, the parent said, "Now you take those tests and *don't put up no fuss,* you hear?"

The same problem may occur sometimes in seeking consent from guardians. When children are cared for by temporary guardians because of their parents' abuse or neglect or when children are under the custody of detention centers, hospitals, or other institutions, one cannot assume automatically that the guardian is in a sufficiently beneficent posture to mitigate the dangers of poor understanding or acquiescent assent by the minor. In at least two ways custodial institutions may create pressure for a minor to assent to research participation.

First, institutions sometimes have reasons to urge minor or adult wards—directly or in subtle ways—to participate in research. Sometimes the institution has a vested interest in the study's results. Other times the staff may wish simply to comply with researchers' requests for subjects, especially when a researcher has a prestigious reputation. Staff even may believe that their institutions' wards have a responsibility to participate in research that will further scientific or other noble objectives. In other words, the custodial guardians' own interests often may create pressures for minors to acquiesce to research requests.

Second, the institution may place no pressure on the minor, but the custodial nature of the minor's circumstance might cause the minor to *perceive* that such pressure exists even when it does not. (For a discussion of sociological research and theory concerning the subtle threats of institutional status upon voluntary consent, see Grisso, in press). Many custodial situations emphasize with minors the importance of obeying institutional rules, and many minors learn that compliance even with the *inferred* desires of staff is the best strategy in order to get along. Under these conditions, the voluntariness of minors' assent to be in research studies has to be questioned.

My research study in the juvenile detention center provides an example for this issue as well. When my group elicited each child's assent to research participation, we carefully explained to him or her that we were not affiliated with the detention center or the court, that they did not have to participate, and that the court would learn nothing about their responses to our questions about them or even whether they had volunteered. Further, our monitoring of the detention center staff indicated that they tried in every way to convey to minors the staff's and the court's disinterest in whether the juveniles participated in the research.

We found, however, that the juveniles were skeptical. Almost all of them that we approached volunteered. But after the research session, we asked them: "Would kids here probably believe us when we tell them that we do not work for the court?" One third of them said most kids would not believe us. On further questioning, about one quarter of them admitted wondering whether we might discuss their participation with the court even though we had guaranteed confidentiality.

Even under these careful conditions, therefore, one must question whether the minors made truly voluntary assent. Our results suggested that a substantial number of them (although not necessarily the majority) complied either as a reflex reaction to obey requests made of them while they were in custody or because they felt that detention staff would react unfavorably to failure to comply. Such institutional effects that jeopardize voluntariness in minors' assent may be quite subtle. One might expect also that the longer a child is dependent on an institution and its staff, the greater the risk of acquiescence to the perceived desires of the caretaker.

In summary, some circumstances that require the permission of parents or of authorized guardians actually may work against the principle of affording protection for children's autonomous assent. These situations raise the possibility that parental or guardian permission is not a reasonable requirement to protect the minor's interests under the circumstances.

Mature minors. Finally, in the last situation, parental participation is superfluous. The commission noted that parental permission might be waived for some research involving "mature minors," for example, adolescents whose capacities to make research decisions are substantially the same as those of most adults. This possibility is most likely to be invoked when the minors are "emancipated." For example, they may be living, working, and perhaps raising families independent of their parents. But it also may be invoked for dependent minors in some research. A number of reviews of adolescents' cognitive and social developmental characteristics (e.g., Weithorn, 1983) have suggested that minors older than 13 may have decision-making capacities similar to those of most adults, at least for purposes of some kinds of research or treatment decisions.

It is not clear, however, why one should consider parental permission to be an *unreasonable* requirement for research involving these minors. The mere fact that they do not *need* protection or that parental permission would be superfluous does not make parental permission unreasonable.

Therefore, it is not clear why "mature minor" status by itself would be a reason to waive the parental permission requirement. On the other hand, the "mature minor" concept may have an important role to play in determining the "appropriate mechanisms" for ensuring minors' protection that researchers are expected to develop whenever they propose to waive the requirement for parental permission on other grounds. Therefore, I now turn to a consideration of those matters.

Substituting "Appropriate Mechanisms"

The DHHS regulations implicitly recognize that when parental and guardian permission will not be obtained, a need arises to take extra steps to protect minors. Whatever these measures are, they should ensure several things: first, that the minors clearly understand the proposed procedures and their purposes; second, that they be in a position to make an autonomous decision to assent or refuse relatively free from conditions that might cause them to volunteer against their will; and third, that they experience similar autonomy in terms of their desires to discontinue participation if that desire should arise.

The text of 46.408 (c) indicates several things to consider: the nature of the procedures that participants will undergo; the risks and benefits; and the age, maturity, status, and conditions of the minors themselves.

No formula can exist for devising or judging the adequacy of special protections to be employed in these situations. Rather than review how each variable might be weighed, I will consider one hypothetical case study to explore the kind of logic that would be required to construct appropriate protective mechanisms when minors' parents and guardians are not involved in the decision. Such a consideration also will provide the context for introducing a few strategies that are not frequently used but that may be encouraged in future research practice.

Imagine that a doctoral candidate wishes to perform research on the cognitive, emotional, and adaptive responses of adolescent females who have decided to obtain abortions. A women's clinic is willing to let the student perform interviews and administer certain paper-and-pencil psychological inventories to adolescent females, ages 13 to 18, at three times: during one of their first counseling visits, immediately after the abortion procedure, and at a follow-up visit to the clinic a few weeks later.

Certain risks and costs accrue to the participants. Some of the questions will focus on personal and sensitive issues, including life circumstances and values involved in the participant's abortion decision. This focus may engender some anxiety by increasing a participant's awareness of her emotional reasons for choosing abortion. Participation will increase one's time at the clinic by a total of about 6 hours across the three research encounters. But whether one assents to or refuses participation will have no effect on the clinic's provision of full services.

Some chance exists of a direct benefit to some of the participants, insofar as self-exploration in the course of answering the researcher's questions may have some positive effect on adaptation. But all clients of the clinic receive counseling from the clinic staff whether or not they participate in the research study.

The research topic and the types of information that its results may provide have important implications for mental health services, cognitive developmental psychology, and law and public policy. The type of information to be obtained could not be acquired from any other population in any other setting.

The clinic is in a state in which adolescent females may legally obtain abortions autonomously and confidentially, and in this clinic, about one half of adolescent females who seek abortion do so without parental knowledge or consent. Requiring parental permission for research participation, therefore, would exclude about one half of the potential sample, including the very adolescents for whom questions of the abortion decision and emotional adaptation are most critical.

Therefore, a situation exists here in which it may be unreasonable to require parental or guardian permission. The parents are unavailable. The research is important for directing policy in the interest of minors similar to those in the study, and it cannot be performed with any other populations. Moreover, the laws of this state allow minors to make the abortion decision and to obtain abortions without parental involvement or awareness.

What remains, therefore, is to ensure that appropriate mechanisms are developed for providing protection that parents normally would be expected to provide in the research permission process.

The researcher might argue that no additional protections are needed because the law already allows adolescents to make independent decisions about this treatment. But this argument should not be accepted. It is true that if adolescents may lawfully seek this treatment independently, probably it is lawful to proceed on the basis of their autonomous assent for low-risk research associated with that treatment. But the mere fact that an action is lawful does not necessarily mean that it is ethical or that it is in the broader best interests of the minors, either as a group or individually. The researcher's obedience to the law is a threshold issue, but does not necessarily satisfy standards for ethical behavior in scientific research, which usually sets a higher standard than legal requirements.

The researcher might argue that no special protections are needed because the prospective participants are "mature minors" who are as capable of understanding the research procedures, risks, and conditions of confidentiality and voluntariness as are adults. The researcher could cite a number of reviews of empirical research and theory, suggesting that adolescents' capacities to understand, reason, and make voluntary decisions in informed consent procedures are not significantly different from those of adults (e.g., Melton, Koocher, & Saks, 1983; Weithorn, 1983). This logic, however, is not persuasive. First, it does not address the fact that heterogeneity is likely to exist in abilities within the adolescent sample, for which reason at least some proportion of the participants may not have abilities that are typical even for the average adolescent. Second, none of the research studies cited in support of the argument have been done with adolescents in such stressful or anxiety-producing circumstances as the abortion process. Stress and anxiety might produce a decrement in functioning, perhaps more for adolescents than for adults.

If past research cannot be used to judge the capacities of the adolescents in the proposed study, one remedy might be to require the researcher to perform what might be called a "pilot assent study." Such a study would include procedures to demonstrate empirically the capacities of the proposed adolescent participants to understand the research procedure when it is presented in the words that will be used to describe it in the actual research study and when offered in the actual social context in which the proposed study will be carried out. In other words, the researcher might be allowed to engage in the assent process with some number of adolescent females visiting the abortion clinic, just as would eventually be done in the study, but without actually engaging in the research procedure with these pilot participants.

This pilot procedure could include a special set of questions that would be asked of the pilot participants after the research procedure has been described to them. This questioning creates a sort of "inform and assess" procedure to determine whether the information actually was understood by the participant. The researcher then could collate the responses obtained from this "pilot assent study" and, if necessary, could revise the assent procedure and wording to improve the participants' understanding. When understanding appears to be adequate for most of the pilot participants, the researcher could present the results to the IRB as documentation that, with this specific participant population and social context, the procedures promote an adequate level of understanding among the adolescents.

Having done this, the researcher has really done four things. First, the procedure has been refined to maximize participants' understanding. Second, the IRB is provided documentation demonstrating that no further protection may be needed to promote understanding. Third, the researcher's piloting of the assent procedure may have discovered information about adolescents' capacities in this setting that in itself furthers knowledge about minors' assent capacities. These results themselves might sometimes be of sufficient importance to be reported in separate publications. Fourth, the researcher has developed an assent procedure that could actually be implemented in the final study. Using this "inform and assess" procedure, when assessment indicates incomplete understanding with a particular adolescent, the researcher can engage in further explanation in order to reach the maximum level of understanding of which a particular participant is capable.

The point of this suggestion is to encourage an empirical approach to providing appropriate mechanisms for protecting minors from their possible deficiencies in understanding. Researchers can and should be much more creative in developing ways to demonstrate empirically that the informing process in assent procedures with minors has achieved its intended purpose.

Additional protection may be needed to ensure that adolescents who are applying for abortions at the clinic are screened initially with regard to their emotional ability to take on the research decision and the research procedure. In addition, one needs to ensure that the adolescent's decision about research participation is not a mere acquiescent response to the researcher's request, that it does not occur under real or imagined pressures by the researcher or the agency, and that the minor feels empowered to withdraw at various stages in the study in the event that she begins to experience it as unduly stressful.

The researcher may argue that supportive assistance to the minor in exercising autonomy on these matters may come from the counseling staff of the abortion clinic itself. Indeed, the commission suggested that nurses or physicians who were unrelated to the research might be enlisted to perform the assent process and perhaps even to be a supportive "escort" for the minor throughout the research process.

Reasons exist, however, for viewing such a plan with skepticism. Whenever minors are in secure custody or hospitalized or even when they are receiving treatment on an outpatient basis, several risks are run by relying on the agency's staff—whether they are doctors, social workers, or anybody else—to provide the advocacy and emotional support that minor research participants might need.

First, the agency itself often has its own interest in the research results and, therefore, in promoting clients' participation. This interest may produce conflicts at times when the minor's independent interests must be encouraged and asserted. Second, even if the agency staff person can set aside competing interests of the agency or has no direct connection to the research itself, the adolescent may not be able to make this distinction. The adolescent needs the agency, the agency's representative is assisting her in the abortion process, and at some point the agency representative is describing the research to her and assisting her in the research decision process. Under these kinds of circumstances, it is not unusual for adolescents and adults alike to assume that a connection exists between the treatment and the research request (Rosen, 1977). One can imagine various presumptions on the part of the minor: "The research must be safe; would the clinic's counselor let me decide by myself, if it were going to be stressful or harmful?" "Might my treatment needs not be met fully if I do not comply with this request?" "The counselor must want me to volunteer; why otherwise would she be asking me to participate?"

For these reasons, screening and advocacy for minors while they are making autonomous decisions about their research participation may often require the added protection afforded by a skilled, supportive person who is allied or associated with neither the researcher nor the agency in which the research is being performed. The screening procedure and role of the advocate would need to be designed clearly by the researcher and taught to the advocate. Beyond this the advocate would carry out the function with special attention to the needs of the adolescents, not the objectives of the researcher or the agency.

In summary, the discussion has highlighted two strategies for providing appropriate protective mechanisms when 46.408 (c) is invoked: empirical documentation of adolescents' understanding, and protections against acquiescence as a consequence of institutional affiliation of the advocate. Surely many other strategies exist; these two were chosen for discussion primarily because neither of them was suggested in the commission's commentary. These strategies may be more or less necessary in various circumstances, and others may have to be created in other circumstances.

In closing, researchers should be aware that 46.408 (c) may have a new application in the 1990s. It is likely that researchers will be dealing with many adolescents who seek HIV testing without parental awareness, and the researchers will want to perform social science research in such circumstances to learn about adolescents' antecedent activities, as well as their behavioral and emotional reactions to their seropositive or negative status. These and other challenges for allowing minors' autonomous assent to research participation are just around the corner.

References

Department of Health and Human Services (DHHS). (1988). *Protection of human subjects, 45 CFR 46.* (originally promulgated 1983). Washington DC: Author.

Grisso, T. (1981). *Juveniles' waiver of rights: Legal and psychological competence.* New York: Plenum.

Grisso, T. (in press). *Voluntary consent to research participation in the institutional context.* In B. Stanley & J. Sieber (Eds.), *Ethical issues in consent to research.* Lincoln: University of Nebraska Press.

Melton, G. (1988). *Ethical and legal issues in research and intervention.* Unpublished paper presented at a workshop on Issues in Prevention and Treatment of AIDS Among Adolescents with Serious Emotional Disturbance, Georgetown University, Washington, DC.

Melton, G., Koocher, G., & Saks, M. (1983). *Children's competence to consent.* New York: Plenum.

National Commission for Protection of Human Subjects of Biomedical and Behavioral Research (NCPHS). (1977). *Report and recommendations: Research involving children* (DHEW Publication No. OS 77-0004). Washington, DC: Government Printing Office.

Rosen, C. (1977). Why clients relinquish their rights to privacy under sign-away pressures. *Professional Psychology, 8,* 17-24.

Weithorn, L. (1983). Involving children in decisions affecting their own welfare: Guidelines for professionals. In G. Melton, G. Koocher, & M. Saks (Eds.), *Children's competence to consent* (pp. 235-260). New York: Plenum.

7

Assent Processes

ALEXANDER J. TYMCHUK

In order to include children and adolescents as participants in social and behavioral research, two levels of individual approval must be obtained: the child or adolescent must assent to the research, and the parent(s) or guardian must give permission. Assent and permission may be distinguished from informed consent. *Informed consent* refers to a process in which a competent adult voluntarily agrees to participate in a research project, based on a full disclosure of pertinent information. *Permission and assent* refer to a parallel process in which the parent or guardian agrees to allow a minor ward to participate in a research project, and the minor child assents or agrees to be a subject in the research. The child may not participate in research without parental permission, and the parent may not "volunteer" the child without the child's approval (except in the case of possible lifesaving experimental therapy that is not available otherwise). Thus, ordinarily, research is permitted only if both agree, and the child has absolute veto power.

As discussed more fully elsewhere (chapters 2, 5, 6 and the Epilogue), two circumstances exist under which the requirement of parental permission may be waived, even in the case of young children: (a) when research involves only minimal risk (no greater than the risks of everyday life) and the research could not practically be carried out without the waiver; and (b) when parental permission will not operate to protect the child, as in the case of abusive or neglectful parents. Other circumstances for which parental permission may be unnecessary are when the minor is married, is a member of the military, or is deemed a mature minor capable of assuming a minimal risk independently. The concept of a "mature minor" is not clearly defined in the law, however, especially with respect to research participation.

Two reasons exist for requiring both parental permission and assent of the minor subject. The first reason pertains mostly to young children and to such special populations as children with mental retardation. Children below a certain age or stage of development are not competent to understand the consequences of participation and to weigh those consequences (Weithorn, 1983). Thus, especially in the case of research involving risk, the permission of a parent or other person who is situated to act in the child's best interests may provide an important safeguard of the child's well-being (Capron, 1982). As Weithorn has shown, however, by mid-adolescence minors have adultlike ability to weigh risks and to consider consequences when deciding whether to participate in research. Hence, in the case of adolescents, a reasonable request for waiver of the parental permission requirement without the appointment of a guardian is likely to be granted, and in any case, the assent procedure would not differ from that used with adults.

The second reason for requiring parental permission has to do with parents' right to have a say in what happens to their children. The reasoning behind this understanding of parental rights is found partly in the fact of parental responsibility for minor children and partly in the fact that 18 is the age of majority for other purposes than research. The age of majority was not based on any empirical determination of when young people acquire mature decision-making skills. With respect to informed consent, the age of majority has been deemed an appropriate boundary because people differ in the rate at which they mature and because it is unclear under what conditions youngsters are capable of making adequate decisions of various kinds (Annas, Glantz, & Katz, 1978).

Under either criterion (immaturity of the child, or right of parents to have a say in what happens to their youngster), the child's assent is a real decision and, as such, should be made under conditions that foster the most competent decision making possible. Parental permission and assent involve the elements of informed consent that, ideally, are presented in a manner entirely appropriate to the circumstances—an ideal that is not always satisfied in the case of children. The purpose of this chapter is to suggest some procedures that might more nearly approach that ideal when the subjects of the research are immature with respect to decision-making ability.

In the case of research procedures that are familiar to the child and that involve no risk, the verbal process administered to each child by the researcher might be as simple and straightforward as the following (adapted from the SUNY Albany IRB recommendations), and be accompanied by a written form communicating the same information:

Do you remember the permission slip you took home for your parents to sign a few days ago?

I am studying how people learn new words. I am asking you and other kids to help me with this project.

If you want to participate, I will need you to help me six times, today, and five more times over the next few weeks. We will work together for about 20 to 30 minutes each time. Each time we will be doing something different, but you shouldn't have any difficulty with any of the things we do. Sometimes we'll ask you to find certain words on a page or to remember letters of words that you see or hear. Other times, I'll ask you to draw some figures, follow directions, tell some stories, and listen to some sentences to tell me what they mean.

This is not a test like you usually have in school. All you have to do is try as hard as you can to do the things I ask and you'll do fine. Your teachers and parents and the other children will not know how well you do. It will be just between you and me and the people I work with.

I would really appreciate it if you would help me to find out about these things, but, if you for some reason feel like you really don't want to do this, just tell me. You may quit at any time.

Do you have any questions? (The researcher should answer any questions the child asks, without discussing specific test items.)

In the case of research that involves any risk or procedures that are unfamiliar to the child, however, the problem is to determine what changes in the consent process might substantially enhance comprehension, competency of decision making, autonomy, and, ultimately, the ability of the child to reach an appropriate decision. This chapter questions the adequacy of the current conceptualization of informed consent. An alternative conceptualization is offered. Finally, ways are suggested to enhance the decision-making capacities of children to assent to research participation, relevant literature is reviewed, and directions for research are indicated.

Questionable Assumptions About Informed Consent

Various difficulties exist with current assumptions about informed consent, especially as they pertain to children and other vulnerable populations. The questionable assumptions are the following:

1. The goal of informing is attained adequately through the present process.
2. One method of administering consent is satisfactory for all people.
3. Subjects understand the information and remember it so that they can use it to decide whether to participate, or later, to decide whether to withdraw.

Contrary to these assumptions, research has demonstrated that competent adults often are inadequately informed under the current process; however, with some changes in the process they can be better informed (Tymchuk, Ouslander, & Rader, 1986; Tymchuk, Ouslander, Rahbar, & Fitten, 1988). Given the difficulties that competent adults have with the usual consent process, informing and obtaining assent from children is even more problematic. It is recognized generally that children's understanding of what is presented during the consent process may be limited by such experimenter-controlled factors as the use of complex and sophisticated language (Grundner, 1980; Jacobs & Tymchuk, 1981).

A related reason that informed consent is sometimes inadequate to the situation is that the consent process as defined by the federal regulations is quite limited. Researchers who follow the regulations then assume that they have done all that is required (Tymchuk & Thompson, 1986). In contrast, when determining whether minors should be given the right to make certain decisions for themselves, the courts apply a more expanded view of consent (Capron, 1982). Before court approval is given in nonresearch settings for limited or full decision making by a minor, the court must be satisfied that the child understands the nature of the procedure being considered, including the risks and benefits of consenting or refusing consent (Capron, 1982). To satisfy the court, there must be some form of assessment of the child's understanding and decision making. These assessments typically use standardized psychological measures presumed to measure understanding and decision making, including intelligence and personality tests (Grisso,

1981) and interviews. Of necessity, these assessments also entail the use of clinical judgment because no standardized scale of general decision making is available and no agreement exists on standards to determine capacity to assent.

An Expanded View of Informed Consent

Informed consent may be viewed within an information-processing framework that involves three distinct phases: input, assimilation, and output (Craik & Lockhart, 1972). Nested within each of these phases are various subcomponents. Table 7.1 shows the various parts of this model and factors that may influence each phase of decision making.

The input phase consists of orientation or preparation for receiving information, perception of the information, discrimination of the various parts of that information, identification of those parts (e.g., words, pictures), and comprehension of what each means. The assimilation phase consists of organizing the information taken in during the input phase, assimilating or integrating it into what the person already knows, and making some evaluation of the importance of that information. The output phase consists of making a decision, maintaining the information for immediate or delayed recall, and applying it as needed in the future.

The expanded view of the consent process has various advantages over the current view. Each phase and its components can be operationalized. Strategies to improve performance of each phase may be developed and tested with specific populations. Such testing could be integral to the consent process with anyone, but most importantly with children. Such assessment would ascertain, for example, what the child sees and hears, what the child understands the material to mean, and whether the child can comprehend what the material signifies about participation in the research. Table 7.2 illustrates such a process.

Various demographic, social, and psychological factors may influence the child's performance at each phase of decision making. All three phases of the consent process may be influenced by the child's age, personality, motivation, values, education (particularly the ability to read), and previous experience (including experience with various types of research and research terminology, or with medical personnel and procedures). Differential experience, even

Table 7.1 Phases of Information Presentation in Decision Making

Input	Assimilation	Output	
		Immediate	*Delayed*
Framework Concepts			
Orientation/Preparation	Prioritizing	Assent	Continued
Perception	Assimilation/	Recall	assent
Discrimination	Integration	Decision	Recall
Identification		making	
Comprehension		Application	
Patient/Subject Variables			
Physical integrity (vision, hearing)			
Personal values/interest			
Previous experience			
Personality			
Mental status			
Memory capacity			
Intelligence			
Age			
Functional/decision making capacity			
Health Professional/Experimenter Variables			
Speed of input	Time allowed	Structured or probed recall	
Method	Training	Definition of being informed	
Single or multiple sense	Aid/Proxy	Criterion level	
Number of trials	Prompting	Prompting	
Size of print/loudness of signal	Correction	Correction	
Position of information			
Massed or distributed			
Conceptual grouping			
Content			
Order of information			
Difficulty			
Training			
Time allowed			
Preparation			
Aid in inputting (e.g., proxy)			

between children of similar ages and particularly between those of different cultures and environments, could account for differences in their understanding of information and in their decision making.

Table 7.2 Suggested Steps for Developing an Assent Process

1. Determine age. If over 18 years, consents by self unless legally determined to be incompetent, in which case legal guardian provides consent while person assents.
2. If under age 18 and an emancipated minor, member of the armed forces, or a mature minor, consents by self.
3. If under age 18, assents, but parent or guardian consents.
4. In order to respect the autonomy and the developing self-determination of a child, effort should be expended to ensure that the child, as well as the parent, understands and utilizes the information.
5. Assess the physical capacity of the child (vision, hearing).
6. Assess child's decision-making capacity or use age as criterion.
7. Assess reading comprehension.
8. Develop consent material (including how comprehension and application are to be assessed) in format and at difficulty level to match child's abilities, ensuring that information contained is identical to that which parent needs.
9. Present information to both child and parent.
10. Assess both child's and parent's comprehension. If parent's is below criterion, provide some alternative procedures, such as the use of repeated trials. If child's is below criterion, consider whether a provision should be made for alternative procedures.
11. Follow up to determine whether their comprehension of the information remains at criterion level and whether they have changed their decision.

A child's performance may be influenced also by experimenter-controlled factors that in turn may be used to enable children to expand their decision-making capacities. These factors include *input* factors, such as the manner, format, complexity, order, conceptual grouping, speed, or amount of information presented. The *assimilation* phase of the consent process may be influenced by the length of time allowed for the individual to process the information, the number of times the information is presented, and whether the experimenter provides corrective or other feedback. The *output* phase may be influenced by such experimenter-controlled factors as the use of prompting or the training of subjects in strategies designed to aid recall or to weigh the decisions (e.g., grouping information or remembering key words.) All of the phases of the consent process may be influenced by the experimenter's use of training, which may include preparing the subject for what is coming, alerting the subject to specific words or phrases, and training the subject in a decision process.

Strategies to Optimize the Informed Consent Process

Drawing on the expanded view of the consent process, I now consider some specific strategies to improve chances that the child is truly informed in the consent process. These strategies include reducing the level of difficulty of information, altering the format of the presentation, and providing training in decision making. The following are examples of the use of such strategies:

Reading level. The difficulty level of the information to be presented should be appropriate to the child's level of ability. Weithorn and Campbell (1982) calibrated the level of difficulty of information so that it would be appropriate for each age level in their study. Tymchuk et al. (1988) expanded on Weithorn and Campbell's procedures by developing vignettes and assessment questionnaires. Because the participants read, on the average, at the fifth-grade level, the material for the simplified presentations was written at that level. Then, to ensure that the information was identical to that in the standard presentation, experts reviewed the simplified materials. Through the use of word-frequency norms, words with low frequency were eliminated. Finally, to ensure that none of the meaning was lost between the standard and simplified versions, each was back-translated from the simplified to the standard. Table 7.3 shows one of the low-risk vignettes on flu vaccination in its standard and simplified formats; Figure 7.1 contains the illustrated format.

Format. Cooke, Tannenbaum, and Gray (1978) found that the average complexity of consent forms ranged from academic to scientific. On the basis of this finding alone, it is illogical to expect children of any age, or even many parents, to understand the contents of such forms.

In only one study was format varied with children (Jacobs & Tymchuk, 1981). In that study, 80 mentally retarded or emotionally disturbed children, representing consecutive admissions to two inpatient wards, were assigned randomly to one of four conditions after having been given the patient's bill of rights in the standard manner. These conditions included presentation of the patient's bill of rights in the standard form or in a simplified form, in storybook form, or in a videotape format. Immediately following admission and presentation of the patient's bill of rights in the standard manner by ward staff, the children, with their assent and parental consent, were asked individually what they thought their rights were while on the ward and then

Table 7.3 Simplified and Standard Formats of Flu Vaccination Vignette

PROBLEM
Let us suppose for a minute that last year you
had the flu. You want to do something so you
will not get the flu again because you know
that it makes you feel sick. The flu would give
you a fever, muscle aches, and a stuffy nose
and throat. You may even get pneumonia
which you can die from.

PROBLEM
Let us suppose that you contracted the flu last
winter and you want to prevent it from
happening again this year because you know
that if you do contract the flu it would not only
make you sick with fever, muscle aches, and
upper respiratory congestion, it may lead to
complications such as pneumonia from which
you could die.

BEST TREATMENT
The best treatment would be to have a flu
vaccination. This would mean getting a small
needle in the arm and giving you the vaccine.
The vaccine would help you not get the flu for
a couple of months. After that you can get a
vaccination every year before the flu season.

DOCTOR PREFERRED TREATMENT
The recommended treatment would be to have
a flu vaccination which would involve the
insertion of a small needle into your upper arm
and injecting the vaccine. Protection from the
vaccine would last a few months and you
would require a vaccination every year before
the flu season.

GOOD THINGS
The one good thing about a flu vaccination is
that after you get it, you would have only a
small chance of getting the flu.

BENEFITS
The major benefit of the flu vaccine is that it is
very likely to prevent you from contracting
current strains of the flu.

BAD THINGS
There are a few bad things that could happen to
you. Your arm might feel sore from the needle.
You might also have some mild flu-like
feelings with a fever and muscle aches. If you
are allergic to eggs, the vaccine might make
you very sick and in rare cases you could die.

RISKS
There would be some risks to having such a
vaccination including some pain for a few days
in your arm where the needle was inserted.
You may also feel some mild flu-like illness
with a fever and muscle aches. More severe
reactions can occur in people who are allergic
to eggs including death in rare cases.

OTHER TREATMENTS
You might not want to have the vaccination.
You would not be protected from the flu then.
But you would avoid some discomforts of the
vaccination. You could still do other things.
You could stay away from people who are
sick. If you are near someone who is sick, you
could wash your hands afterwards. This would
help, but not as much as the vaccine.

ALTERNATIVE
You may choose not to have the vaccination.
This would leave you less protected against
current virus strains but would spare you some
possible mild discomfort of the vaccination.
Close attention to avoiding people who are ill
and careful handwashing after such contacts
might improve your protection, but probably to
a lesser extent than vaccination.

answered a set of true/false questions about those rights. The results
showed clearly that the standard presentation did little to inform the
youngsters who, on the average, could remember fewer than one of
their rights. After the second presentation in any one of the four formats, a significant improvement occurred; the four formats were
equally effective, suggesting that repeated presentations of information may improve understanding.

Let us suppose last year you got the flu and it made you very sick. You had a fever, muscle aches and a stuffy nose and throat. You know that you could also get pneumonia from which you could die.

So you want to do something so that you will not get the flu again this year.

The best thing to do is to get a flu vaccination. This means getting a small needle in the arm and giving you the vaccine. The vaccine will help protect you for a couple of months. After that you can get a vaccination every year before the flu season.

The good thing about the vaccination is that there will only be a small chance of getting the flu after the vaccination.

There may be a few bad things that might happen to you. Especially if you are allergic to eggs, you might become very sick and in rare cases die after getting the vaccination.

You might have some mild flu like symptoms with fever and muscle aches after the vaccination.

Your arm might feel sore from the needle.

You might not want to have the vaccination. You will not be protected from the flu then. But, you will avoid the pain of the shot or the flu like symptoms.

You can still do other things like staying away from people who are sick.

If you are near someone who is sick, you should wash your hands afterwards. This would help but not as much as the vaccination.

Figure 7.1. Illustrated Format of Flu Vaccination Vignette

SOURCE: From "Optimizing the Informed Consent Process with Elderly People" by A. J. Tymchuk and J. G. Ouslander, 1990, *Educational Gerontology, 16* (3), pp. 245-255. Copyright 1990 by Hemisphere Publishing Corporation. Reprinted by permission.

Training. No attempts have been made to examine the effects of training on acquisition and understanding of information, decision making, or the appropriateness of decision making by children. It is well understood in the fields of education and psychology that training can improve skills. The understanding of information, the use of decision-making skills, and the making of appropriate decisions are all skills that may be developed through training.

It has been suggested that the ability to carry out a decision rationally does not appear until about age 14 (Weithorn & Campbell, 1982). Yet, components of the process occur in very young children who recognize basic if/then situations. If decision skills were trained actively in children, then perhaps they would develop well before age 14. Research has demonstrated that young children can recognize, understand, and process information in contexts similar to informed consent contexts. Poche, Brouwer, and Swearington (1981), for example, trained three intellectually normal children aged 3 to 5 to recognize inappropriate behavior in an adult (behavior typical of child molesters), to act on that information to prevent their being molested, and to generalize this training with one adult to a different adult in another situation. This training occurred rapidly and effectively, and the results were maintained over time. Similar results have been achieved with preschoolers in teaching them to make emergency phone calls (Jones & Kazdin, 1980) and with preadolescent "latch-key" children between the ages of 8 and 10, concerning what they should do while at home and unsupervised (Peterson, 1984).

Although many successful efforts have been made to develop basic skills in children and in mentally retarded adults, few efforts have been made to teach higher order skills.

Conclusion

The goal of informed consent has been met imperfectly with all populations, but especially with children. The quality and character of persons' decision processes differ. Thus, instead of one process of administering informed consent (or assent) for all, individually determined consent procedures are needed. Various educational strategies might enable researchers to fulfill the goal of consent. These strategies, although still not fully developed, appear to have important implications for enlarging our understanding of children's capabilities to assent to research participation.

References

Annas, G., Glantz, L., & Katz, B. (1978). The law of informed consent in human experimentation: Institutionalized mentally inform. In National Commission for the Protection of Human Subjects of Biomedical and Behavioral Research, *Research
involving those institutionalized as mentally infirm* (Appendix; DHEW Publication
No. OS 78-007). Washington, DC: Government Printing Office.

Capron, A. (1982). The competence of children as self-deciders in biomedical interventions. In W. Gaylin & R. Macklin (Eds.), *Who speaks for the child: The problem of
proxy consent* (pp. 57-114). New York: Plenum.

Cooke, R., Tannenbaum, A., & Gray, B. (1978). A survey of institutional review boards
and research involving human subjects. In the National Commission for the Protection of Human Subjects of Biomedical and Behavioral Research, *Appendix to report
and recommendations on institutional review boards.* (DHEW Publication No. OS
78-0009). Washington, DC: Government Printing Office.

Craik, F., & Lockhart, R. (1972). Levels of processing: A framework for memory research. *Journal of Verbal Learning and Verbal Behavior, 11,* 671-684.

Grisso, T. (1981). *Juveniles' waiver of rights: Legal and psychological competence.*
New York: Plenum.

Grundner, T. (1980). On the readability of surgical consent forms. *New England Journal of Medicine, 302,* 900-902.

Jacobs, C., & Tymchuk, A. (1981). *Informed consent with children.* Paper presented at
the annual meeting of the American Association on Mental Deficiency, Detroit.

Jones, R., & Kazdin, A. (1980). Teaching children how and when to make emergency
telephone calls. *Behavior Therapy, 11,* 509-521.

Peterson, L. (1984). Teaching home safety and survival skills in latchkey children.
Journal of Applied Behavioral Analysis, 17, 279-294.

Poche, C., Brouwer, R., & Swearington, M. (1981). Teaching self-protection to young
children. *Journal of Applied Behavioral Analysis, 14,* 169-176.

Tymchuk, A., Ouslander, J., & Rader, N. (1986). Informing the elderly: A comparison
of four methods. *Journal of the American Geriatric Society, 34,* 818-822.

Tymchuk, A., Ouslander, J., Rahbar, B., & Fitten, J. (1988). Medical decision making
among elderly people in long term care (Special issue). *Gerontologist, 28.*

Tymchuk, A., & Thompson, J. (1986). Academic senate members' knowledge of and
attitudes toward human subject protection guidelines. *Psychological Reports, 59,*
323-328.

Weithorn, L. (1983). Children's capacities to decide about participation in research.
IRB: A Review of Human Subjects Research, 5, 1-5.

Weithorn, L., & Campbell, S. (1982). The competency of children and adolescents to
make informed treatment decisions. *Child Development, 53,* 1589-1598.

PART III

Research on High-Risk Behavior

8

Protecting Children's Rights in AIDS Research

MARY JANE ROTHERAM-BORUS
CHERYL KOOPMAN

For the last two years, we have conducted an AIDS prevention program with adolescents who are engaged in high-risk sexual and drug-
use behaviors. In the course of this work, our staff has been confronted
frequently with ethical problems requiring the application of the Office for Protection from Research Risks (OPRR) guidelines to sophisticated and complex dilemmas. This chapter reviews these dilemmas as
they have presented themselves in the lives of our clients. Generally,
these brief case studies suggest three major ethical issues that must be
addressed by all researchers in this area:

1. Consent. When is it necessary to obtain parental consent for the conducting of research with children?
2. Confidentiality. What criteria determine when clinical concerns override
   concerns for confidentiality?
3. Intervention. Whose views determine the ethical guidelines for
   designing AIDS prevention and intervention programs?

The ethical framework that has guided our field decisions is summarized by Walters (1988), who suggests the following criteria for

AUTHORS' NOTE: This work was supported by Grant No. 1P50 MH 43520 to the HIV
Center for Clinical and Behavioral Studies from the National Institutes of Mental Health and
the National Institute on Drug Abuse. We are also thankful to Ruth Macklin, Judy Long, Anke
A. Ehrhardt, Clara Haignere, Laurie Nathan, and Judith Rabkin for their contributions.

evaluating research policies regarding HIV infection: (a) the potential benefits and risks of a particular choice, (b) the fairness of the distribution of the outcomes to different groups, and (c) the rights of those affected. The application of these criteria often demands difficult tradeoffs, choosing a course of action that optimizes on some criteria at the expense of others. Ethical dilemmas vary considerably. Each new problem requires reconsideration of these criteria in an attempt to optimize along each dimension.

When Is Parental Consent Necessary?

Vignette One. A runaway female adolescent was recruited into a longitudinal study while she was living on her own and was, therefore, considered a mature minor in New York State. Later, she returned to her parents' home. Does the researcher then need parental consent to continue following her? The father does not know the girl is participating in research. What if he tells the researcher, "Leave my child alone?" Should the researcher continue to follow her?

Vignette Two. A researcher wants to conduct research in a community-based clinic with 12- to 17-year-old males who self-identify as homosexual and engage in high-risk, unprotected sexual intercourse with men. Most of the youths live at home; however, their parents generally do not know of their children's sexual preference. Is parental consent needed to conduct an AIDS prevention program with these gay youth?

Vignette Three. An AIDS prevention program is being evaluated in a school district. Some parents do not want their children to participate. Is it ethical to circumvent parental consent by referring potential participants to the school nurse or to a clinic setting where parental consent would not be required?

Vignette Four. A 17-year-old male living at home is participating in AIDS prevention research. Parental consent was obtained for program participation. HIV testing was not part of the research protocol. Now, the youth discloses high-risk sexual behavior, wants HIV testing, and does not want his parents to know. Is it ethical to provide the youth with information about how to obtain clinical services delivering HIV testing without seeking his parents' consent?

In each of these dilemmas, the researcher must decide when it is necessary to seek parental consent for doing research with youth.

Two decades ago, adolescents were assumed to have no rights to represent themselves (Goldstein, Freud, & Solnit, 1980). Today, however, exceptions and guidelines exist (OPRR, 1983) that identify circumstances requiring parental consent and specify standards for designing a consent form. Where a researcher is conducting a low-risk survey, it is unnecessary to obtain parental consent (OPRR, 1983). *Low risk* is defined by the following criteria: (a) no sensitive information is elicited; (b) anonymity of responses is assured by the procedures; or (c) no subjects' responses could place them in jeopardy of criminal or civil liability or hurt their financial standing or employability.

Typically, however, parental permission is required for youth under 18 years of age. Strictly speaking, such permission is a preliminary requirement for participation in research: the minor still has the right to "assent" or "refuse" (chapter 6). Exceptions exist, however, for "mature minors," although it may be ethically desirable to obtain parental consent in most cases even if it is not required (chapter 6).

Despite the apparent clarity of the OPRR guidelines, AIDS research raises a number of questions. These OPRR guidelines provide one framework to help guide decision making, but ethical criteria may lead to alternative solutions to these decisions.

Shifting Youth Status

One kind of ethical challenge is presented when the adolescent's status shifts during a research protocol: what kinds of shifts affect the parents' right to consent to their child's participation? Ethically, potential benefits to the youth and the right of adolescents to self-determination have to be weighed against parental rights.

When the youth's status is no longer that of an emancipated minor, as in Vignette One when the participant returned home, the parents have the right to refuse consent. Parental consent could be obtained, however, in a manner that takes the rights and needs of the youth into consideration. Youths who have lost their status as emancipated minors may be asked to release information informing their parents of their participation in a research protocol. The parents of those who agree may be informed about the nature of the study and its potential risks and benefits. Then, an attempt may be made to elicit parental consent.

Ethical criteria for defining *emancipated* or *mature youth status* in a particular situation are not always obvious. For example, in Vignette

Two, in which a community agency already has defined the status of participants as "mature minors," it may not be ethically necessary to obtain parental consent for these gay youth. The community agency has defined these youth as mature minors and has thereby limited harm that might result from providing parents with information about their child's sexual orientation, such as parental rejection of that child (Martin & Hetrick, 1988). When a researcher confronts the tension between the parents' rights to consent and the potential risks and benefits to the youth, an ethical resolution may be to accept the community agency's determination of mature youth status and seek agency consent for the research protocol in lieu of parental consent.

Weighing Clinical Concerns for Youth Against Parents' Rights

Another kind of ethical challenge is presented when clinical concerns for the youth clash with the parents' rights to consent to their child's participation in research. The tension may be resolved by separating clinical concerns from research concerns. One resolution to the dilemma of Vignette Three is to refer youths to the school nurse without enrolling the youth in the study. The referral is processed as one for medical services, not as part of a research protocol. This resolution gives the greatest weight to protecting the health of the adolescents; by refusing enrollment in the study, however, consideration is shown also for the parents' rights.

More decisive action is appropriate, however, in research programs that offer treatment. For example, if an HIV-positive youth wants to participate in a drug treatment study but the parents refuse consent, the researcher has an obligation to help secure a court order to allow treatment, although this help does not require enrolling the youth in any accompanying research. Because adolescents can consent to clinical services, it does not necessarily follow that they can consent to research.

HIV Testing as a Special Case of Consent

Parental consent has been obtained for participation in AIDS prevention research. Must consent also be obtained for an HIV test if it was not part of the original research protocol? This situation was presented in Vignette Four. HIV testing raises special issues involving consent, and no answers are clear-cut. Individual, highly subjective judgments are involved in evaluating the benefits and risks likely to ensue if negative HIV serostatus is established. Therefore, difficult ethical decisions arise concerning the weight to be given to parents' rights.

The youth's right to seek testing must be balanced against the parents' rights to participate in the decision. An emphasis on the parents' rights, however, assumes that promoting the children's well-being is the major consideration in consenting to medical services. We take issue with this position. The main justification for considering the parents' "right" to decide on their child's behalf is that the child may not be developmentally capable of making the best decision on his or her behalf and that the parents are in a better position to represent their child's views (Capron, 1982). Seeking parental consent for HIV testing may lead to unintended consequences for the child. Parents who learn of their child's seropositivity may unintentionally jeopardize a child's admission to special treatment programs. For example, in a recent Florida case, a 14-year-old girl was denied admission to a home for mentally disturbed youth after her mother revealed her seropositivity.

In New York, the law does not distinguish between youths and adults as to who may decide to take a test. Therefore, a youth must be able to deliberate the risks and benefits of being tested. If an adolescent is able to anticipate the consequences of testing, parental consent is not required for making a clinical referral. Furthermore, disclosure and counseling is required by law, so the adolescent will be assisted in his or her deliberations.

If HIV testing is not part of the protocol but the youth requests testing during the course of the research, the researcher ethically could provide information about HIV testing without the parents' consent. This is analogous to providing information about how to get tested for other sexually transmitted diseases without parental consent. Even though the situation is analogous, ethical and legal considerations specific to HIV testing may lead to a different decision. Conducting HIV testing has more ethical problems associated with it than the decision to provide general information on testing or counseling for a sexually transmitted disease.

Several reasons are presented for being concerned about whether providing test results could heighten the risk of suicide. First, adolescent thinking is characterized by cognitive impulsivity and a sense of invulnerability (Elkind, 1967; Urberg & Robins, 1983). Death often is not seen as permanent by adolescents. Suicidal adolescents sometimes view death as a reversible event and perceive suicide as a means of getting even with others. Second, youth living under such stressful conditions as homelessness may be particularly vulnerable to depression and suicide attempts when burdened with further stress. As many as 15% of males and 44% of females living in inner-city shelters meet DSM-III criteria for a diagnosis of depressive disorder (Shaffer & Caton, 1984). Furthermore, we have found in preliminary analysis of interviews with inner-city youth that 17% of the runaway males, 23% of the runaway females, and 43% of the gay male adolescents reported that they have attempted suicide. Third, an increased rate of suicide among AIDS patients has been noted (Marzuk et al., 1988), raising the issue of whether knowledge of HIV status increases suicidal behavior.

Due to these consideration, disclosing HIV test results to youth, whether in the context of research or clinical practice, requires evaluating the youth's cognitive and emotional capability to project the consequences of testing and to think rationally about these consequences without bringing harm to the self or others. This evaluation needs to consider factors associated with such particular settings and populations as homelessness and homosexuality. At one agency serving homeless youth in New York City, only 6 of 211 youth who presented themselves for HIV testing actually were tested after being evaluated for their ability to understand and cope with the consequences of knowing their results.

The strongest argument in favor of enabling youth to learn their HIV status is that existing drugs can substantially alleviate symptoms and prolong the lives of HIV-infected persons (Kolata, 1989). To enable youths to benefit from taking these drugs, however, necessitates that they first get tested and be informed of their results. Inadequate research exists to determine the most ethical resolution of the conflict between the risks of increasing the chances of suicide if youths learn their seropositivity status versus the risk of avoidable illness and death from AIDS if youths are not informed. Researchers must set criteria for adolescents' participation in protocols regarding HIV testing without the benefit of adequate evidence to guide them.

Ethical procedures must include adequate counseling and follow-up to help people cope with test results without bringing harm to themselves or to others. In settings where youths obtain HIV testing on their own initiative, research protocols need to be designed that take advantage of information that can be garnered from these naturally occurring experiments.

Confidentiality: When Do Clinical Concerns Take Precedence?

Vignette Five. A 16-year-old runaway girl is recruited into research. She is prostituting and using cocaine, crack, marijuana, and alcohol on a daily basis. Does good clinical care of her research participation and of her high-risk behaviors demand disclosure to the community agency providing shelter and social services to this youth?

Vignette Six. You responded to a situation similar to Vignette Four (a male adolescent who has engaged in high-risk sexual behavior requests testing) by referring the boy to an anonymous testing site. He discloses his seropositive status to you. State law mandates that you place this information in his medical chart. Do you have a responsibility to inform his parents?

Vignette Seven. A study is conducted on HIV-positive mothers and their babies. The intervention includes assistance in foster care placement for the mothers who choose this. At birth, all babies will test HIV positive. Later, only 25% to 50% will continue to test HIV positive (Bayer, 1989). Do you inform the social service agency involved in the placement process about these babies' HIV status? If the state requires disclosure of HIV status to the social service agency, as is the case in New York, should HIV testing of the babies be avoided so that no results will have to be disclosed?

Vignette Eight. A researcher is conducting an ethnographic study of needle sharing among IV drug users. The HIV status of the research participants has been assessed. In the natural setting, the researcher observes behaviors of many who have not given consent and whose serostatus is, therefore, unknown. The estimated risk of infection on a single needle sharing is 1% (D. Des Jarlais, personal communication, March 16, 1989). What should the researcher do if an HIV-positive youth shoots drugs and then passes the needle to a person whose HIV status is unknown?

Weighing Clinical Concerns Against Respecting Confidentiality

Issues of confidentiality are related often to issues of consent. Clinical concerns may override concerns for confidentiality even when a youth is evaluated as sufficiently mature to provide informed consent without parental consent. Particularly when doing research with children and adolescents, the researcher is required ethically to disclose confidential information about the youth if the researcher deems that overriding the youth's rights to confidentiality is necessary to protect the youth or others from harm. Children and adolescents are assumed to be underdeveloped in their ability to make decisions in their best interests. For youths engaging in self-destructive behavior, the threshold for overriding confidentiality is very low. Disclosing information, however, is not always the best way to help protect the youth from harm. In the arena of AIDS research, the disclosure of HIV-related information has more dire potential consequences than other information that is likely to be obtained in research.

In Vignette Five, respect for the girl's autonomy must be weighed against the likely consequences of her high-risk behavior (Silber, 1987). Such dilemmas can be anticipated by researchers by specifying in the informed consent process the specific behaviors that may be disclosed to others. Whether the need for clinical intervention overrides the commitment to confidentiality depends on the agency, the presence of parental guidance, and the youth's age, risk behavior, and serostatus.

The agency. The kind of agency plays a key role in this issue. Protocols instituted in schools are quite different from those instituted in a drug rehabilitation program. The decision to disclose in a community setting is limited typically to "dangerous" acts. The definition of *dangerous* depends on the perceived liability of the agency and well-being of the youth.

Presence of parental guidance. When youth are in the care of their parents, stronger grounds exist for disclosing youths' behavior to parents than otherwise. The right to information regarding potential danger could be specified in the consent procedure with parents. The parents have a primary obligation to prevent harm to their children. Therefore, they have the right to be informed if researchers believe the child is in danger. In contrast, much less justification exists for disclosure to parents regarding potential danger when parents already have ceased taking care of their child.

Age. Dramatic differences occur from early to late adolescence. Older adolescents are more capable of giving adequate consideration to the potential risks and benefits of their behavior than younger adolescents. Therefore, the researcher is more likely to feel obligated to disclose the potentially dangerous behavior of younger children than of older children.

Risk behavior. Different behaviors suggest different degrees of risk. Drinking alcohol once a month does not constitute a serious or dangerous act that must be disclosed for the well-being of a youth. In contrast, sexual abuse must always be reported. The behavior of a gay youth at high risk for contracting HIV due to his behavior is less easily assessed. One must consider the potential harm to both the research process, and to the youths, in any decision to disclose. As an alternative to reporting, the researcher might attempt to convince the youth to seek help with high-risk behaviors although, if this effort is unsuccessful, the dilemma remains.

HIV Testing and Confidentiality

The possibility that youths participating in research may obtain HIV testing opens up a number of confidentiality issues. If the youth is seropositive, breaches of confidentiality may produce many negative outcomes, including job discrimination, the inability to obtain life or health insurance, or difficulty in foster care placement. Furthermore, as soon as information about a youth's serostatus is disclosed, the researcher loses control over its consequences. A seropositive youth may disclose his or her serostatus to persons who will not respond with appropriate concern for his or her well-being and rights. For example, a youth may tell friends and teachers who in turn tell others, resulting in social ostracism of the youth.

What happens when a major clinical concern arises for these young people? Let us assume, for example, that a youth in Vignette Two (gay male adolescent participating in AIDS prevention program without parental consent) is HIV positive and beginning to be symptomatic. The determination has been made that this youth is a mature minor, independent of the need for parents to consent to his participation in an AIDS prevention program. The case must be reevaluated, however, now that the youth is known to be HIV positive. Because such drug treatments as AZT can prolong life (Kolata, 1989), substantial clinical care can be made available to this youth. If such a drug intervention as AZT is being recommended for clinical trials, the treatment of a life-threatening illness becomes a major ethical responsibility to this youth.

Should parents be notified in such circumstances even if the youth resists? Parents will learn about their son's HIV infection once he begins to show symptoms of AIDS, although this may not occur for several years. The pivotal consideration in deciding whether the parents should be informed about their son's HIV status is the likely outcome of the parents learning sooner rather than later. Thus, in many cases, disclosure is indicated.

Recent legislation may create the opportunity for natural experiments. For example, New York recently passed a statute, N.Y. A.#9765-A (1989), allowing physicians to disclose serostatus to parents or guardians of HIV-positive youth when necessary for care or treatment unless the youth already has the legal authority to consent to health care (Greater New York Hospital Association, 1988). This statute also makes it mandatory that HIV status must be recorded in all medical records when it is known. It may only be disclosed, however, under certain circumstances. Therefore, once consent for testing is obtained, confidentiality issues are determined theoretically by the requirements of this statute. Despite the good intentions of such legislation, its effects on confidentiality in practice must be investigated. The potential harmful consequences inherent in disclosure, such as school discrimination, have not been studied adequately. Researchers must examine decision makers' (physicians' and nurses') base rates for disclosing serostatus in particular kinds of situations and the resulting benefits and risks.

Are the criteria different for obtaining consent for HIV testing when potential negative consequences may occur as a result of institutional tracking? Youths receiving parental care generally stay in their parents' care, but institutionalized youth are likely to be moved repeatedly. Information about HIV status is usually available to institutions making admission and placement decisions. In some states, such as New York, once consent has been granted to test a youth in foster care, it is mandatory that the youth's HIV status be noted in the youth's foster care records. HIV assessment deserves special consideration if the youth is institutionalized or at risk of institutionalization.

When the babies' initial HIV status is disclosed in Vignette Seven, the rights of persons assisting in the babies' care are maintained. Furthermore, benefits accrue to the HIV-positive babies, because more appropriate care can be provided. Disclosure of babies' status to foster care institutions is required by New York law. What is legally required, however, may have ethical problems associated with it. Revealing the babies' HIV status may harm those babies who will eventually prove HIV negative if this information jeopardizes the babies' placement in a foster home. Because some foster homes are willing to accept HIV-positive babies, systematic data are needed for evaluating the risk of disclosure hindering placement in foster care. Such risks need to be weighed in conjunction with potential benefits and individual rights that are also considerations in this vignette. Disclosure seems the best decision here, because the demands of caring for HIV-positive babies merit extra consideration for the rights of caretakers and foster parents. The harm to HIV-negative babies can be minimized when social service staff and foster parents are informed that 50% to 75% of the babies eventually will test HIV negative. Furthermore, education on the low risk of HIV infection from casual contact minimizes harm to HIV-positive babies. These considerations also justify the decision to test the babies in the first place.

Special Problems Raised in Ethnographic Research

Ethnographic research offers the advantage of observing actual behavior associated with HIV transmission, but ethnography also raises issues involving both consent and confidentiality. How does the question of who gives consent in an ethnographic study affect confidentiality? The potential for tension between confidentiality and clinical concerns is immense. Because the behaviors observed in ethnographic research are often socially unacceptable, illegal, and dangerous, the potential for great harm exists both from inappropriate disclosure and from failure to disclose to persons at risk.

In Vignette Eight (in which an HIV-positive person passes a needle to an HIV-negative person), intervention seems required in observing a highly risky act. Stopping the needle sharing, however, could disclose simultaneously serostatus to all participants in the setting. It is unclear how high the risk of infection must be before confidentiality is violated. For example, if the estimated rate of infection was .1% or .01%, rather than 1%, would this alter the researchers' decision?

Such situations must be anticipated in the drafting of the informed consent agreement. The risk of breaching confidentiality regarding the HIV status of participants must be minimized. Agreements can inform participants of the limits to confidentiality in advance. For example, participants can be informed in advance that the researchers will intervene when needle sharing occurs.

Alternatively, the study could be designed to keep the observer blind as to the serostatus of the participants but include education for participants about the dangers of sharing needles and how to sterilize needles. Of course, efforts must be made to account for the effects of any intervention on the events observed (Schatzman & Strauss, 1973).

The Intervention: Whose Views Determine the Goals and Tactics?

Vignette Nine. A researcher is designing an AIDS prevention module with adolescents who attend a community program. Roughly one half of the adolescents have experienced sexual intercourse. Is sexual abstinence the only message that may be delivered?

Vignette Ten. Researchers are considering the use of graphic comic books to eroticize safer sex—to encourage youths to substitute safer sex for high risk sex. Should such graphic materials be made available to youths?

The researcher designing an intervention is confronted with decisions about the rights of different players: the youths, their parents, agency staff, research team, and the larger lay community. For example, the researcher is likely to confront disparities between the norms of the larger community and those of a community agency in which youths are recruited into research. Some communities never perceive consensual sexual activity between two adults or adolescents of the same sex to be an acceptable life-style choice, yet the goal of some community agencies is to facilitate healthy adjustment of those who have chosen such a life-style.

Abstinence is generally the only community norm encouraged for youth, with many persons in the 1980s having voiced sharp disapproval of premarital sexual activity among adolescents (Hayes, 1987), yet sexually active youths ignore this norm and put themselves at risk for contracting AIDS by engaging in unprotected sexual intercourse. Ethical tension in Vignette Nine occurs between respecting a youth's right to make sexual decisions versus respecting the community's rights to reinforce norms about sexuality.

Describing the benefits of abstinence while also presenting a range of alternatives that can reduce the likelihood of infection may resolve this conflict. The government and schools have endorsed the prevention message "Just say *no!*" Evidence in the smoking and drug prevention literature, however, shows that adolescents do not have the social skills to resist peer pressure (Botvin, Baker, Fizazzola, & Millman, 1984; Botvin, Eng, & Williams, 1980; Jessor, Chase, & Donovan, 1980). Teenage pregnancy prevention efforts relying on the "Just say no" approach have also clearly failed in this country in comparison with the more realistic approaches used in other developed countries (Dryfoos, 1985).

When the rights of youth to receive information about sex are pitted against the rights of the parents and the community to restrict such exposure, the researcher may assume youths that have the right to information so that they can protect themselves. How is the researcher's decision affected by the realization that the youths are under the protection of their parents and communities, which have the responsibility for guiding sexual behavior?

If the community advocates abstinence, researchers adopting a position of modifying existing sexual habits are attacked as the "Pied Pipers of Sex" (Welbourne-Moglia & Edwards, 1986). This criticism comes not from fringe segments of the populations but from middle America. Although the abstinence message typifies the far right, particularly the fundamentalist religious groups in this country, it also characterizes the position taken by the New York public schools, New York State, the National Institute on Drug Abuse, and the Centers for Disease Control.

Despite the current conservative view adopted by government, 80% of American adults surveyed in a recent study approve of providing sex education to youth (Gallup Poll, 1980). Furthermore, 83% of parents surveyed support having AIDS education in public schools (Korcock, 1987). Such general data, however, do not specify the goals and strategies of such programs. Researchers must make difficult decisions in specifying these goals and strategies.

We believe two factors to be fundamental in deciding how much weight to give to the views of the various decision-making bodies: (a) the population to be studied, and (b) the community that is responsible for that subpopulation of youth.

The Population to Be Studied

A key characteristic to consider in designing an intervention is the degree of risk of AIDS among targeted adolescents. A seropositivity rate of .02% in a population warrants a different intervention from one of 50%. If the seropotivity rate is extremely high, ethical concerns for minimizing the risk of contracting infection are primary. It appears that switching to low-risk sexual activities has reduced effectively the incidence of high-risk sex among gay adults (Martin, 1987).

Evidence that the onset of intercourse can be delayed by encouraging low-risk behaviors comes from research showing that sexual development of white females typically follows a sequence (e.g., first holding hands, then kissing, then breast fondling, then genital petting, and finally intercourse; Vener & Stewart, 1974).

Where the seropositivity rate is low, ethical concerns, such as respecting the rights of the community to guide the sexual development of its youth, must be considered. Should a person's race make a difference in deciding whether to encourage masturbation and petting? The answer is not clear. Black youth do not proceed typically along the same route of sexual milestones as do white females (Belcastro, 1985; Hayes, 1987). Encouraging black youth to adopt this "white route" may affect the development of ethnic identity. Religious norms also clash with the decision to encourage masturbation and petting. For example, masturbation is considered sinful by Roman Catholics and Orthodox Jews (Gregersen, 1986). In minimizing the potential for harm from AIDS and the potential harm to ethnic identity, we have elected to discuss masturbation and petting as alternatives that some people choose as a substitute for sexual intercourse, while neither encouraging or discouraging youth from engaging in these activities.

One must consider also the proportion of youth in a target population who are sexually active (Rotheram-Borus, Koopman, & Bradley, 1988). The goal of a program for sexually inactive youth is clearly to slow down or prevent the onset of high-risk sexual behavior (Hayes, 1987). For sexually active youth the goal is to reduce or eliminate high-risk behavior by substituting safer behaviors. It is more difficult to change behavior once it is initiated than it is to delay its onset (Flora & Thoresen, 1988; Jessor, Donovan, & Widmer, 1980). Therefore, targeting sexually active youth is likely to require a greater investment of resources than targeting inactive youth. Because younger adolescents are more likely to be sexually inactive, an intervention that delays the onset of sexual intercourse is more likely to benefit younger rather than older adolescents.

Ideally, everyone should receive adequate AIDS prevention help. Resources for prevention, however, are limited. Therefore, in practice, choices are made between providing help to fewer youths at higher risk or to more youths at lower risk. The severity of need and the number of youths served may influence the choice. For example, youth living in social service care become sexually active at younger ages than other youth (Hein et al., 1978). Therefore, they needs AIDS prevention sooner. Because this sexual behavior is difficult to change, a high investment of resources per youth is required, with fewer youths served per dollar spent.

Identifying the Community Responsible for a Youth Population

The community responsible for the well-being and development of a population of youth should influence the design of any AIDS prevention intervention. For example, an intervention designed for a school is usually less explicit than it would be in most community agencies serving youth (e.g., a YMCA). Typically, consideration is given to the norms of the community and the organization within which the research is being conducted. Norms regarding sexuality and illicit drug use evolved before AIDS became the epidemic that it is today; hence, community norms often clash with the content and explicitness of interventions designed to prevent youth from contracting AIDS. For example, it is difficult to discuss avoiding the exchange of bodily fluids without mentioning words such as *penis* or *vagina* (Whyte, 1987). Such explicit discussion may be viewed as offensive by some members of a community.

The decision to use graphic materials about safer sex techniques illustrates these concerns. In our research, we decided against distributing erotic comic books to adolescents partly because we felt that other adults in the community (parents, teachers, and counselors) would be offended by the graphic portrayal of sex in the materials. We relied on less graphic information, thus balancing consideration of the rights of the community to guide the sexual development of its youth with the youth's right to information about safer sexual behavior.

Recommendations

Train Staff to Make Ethical Decisions in Field Settings

Research staff face unanticipated ethical decisions in field settings. These decisions require a comprehensive understanding of the ethical guidelines regarding consent and confidentiality. Staff must be trained to prepare for these decisions. It is important to hold workshops for staff and supervisors to review decision making regarding ethical issues likely to arise in the field. The use of provocative and controversial vignettes is very helpful in such training.

Logs of critical incidents may be established and reviewed by re-search supervisors and community agencies. Logging these incidents ensures monitoring for potential conflicts of interest or unethical con-duct and provides documentation regarding potential liability. Be-cause no researcher can anticipate the breadth or nature of the challenges to confidentiality, these logs help researchers evolve more comprehensive policies.

If good reasons exist to question whether the research process poses too much risk for a given population, open-ended interviews of research participants can identify such negative consequences (e.g., concerns about confidentiality of the information elicited). Such in-terviews constitute a *study within a study* and place a substantial bur-den on the research effort. They can alleviate concerns, however, that cannot be adequately dismissed without further information (Carter & Deyo, 1981).

Anticipate Ethical Dilemmas

In designing consent forms, it is important to anticipate what risk behaviors may occur. Participants must be informed of the specific behaviors that will be disclosed for the purpose of enabling responsi-ble adults to help youth or to protect others.

Secure Consent Whenever Possible

It is usually necessary to secure several levels of consent when conducting field research with youth, including the consent of the youth, community agency staff, and parents. For minors, parental consent is typically required, except when the potential negative consequences of securing parental consent will jeopardize the health and well-being of the participant—often a difficult judg-ment. When emancipated or mature minors return to living with parents, their parents' rights for informed consent are reactivated. Institutions and social welfare agencies with responsibilities for ensuring the well-being of youth in their care also have rights to informed consent, which must be balanced with the well-being of youths participating in research.

Take Special Precautions to Protect Confidentiality

The more sensitive or intimate the revealed information, the greater the responsibility for confidentiality (Cook, 1976). In AIDS treatment or prevention research, highly sensitive and intimate data usually are obtained; however, AIDS research may bring other values into conflict with the participant's right to privacy (Cook, 1976).

When research addresses high-risk behaviors with potential implications for legal, psychiatric, and medical care, it is critical to obtain federal certificates of confidentiality to protect the participants. A certificate, however, is not an absolute guarantee of confidentiality, as information that can lead to great harm may have to be reported (Walters, 1988). The possibility that sensitive information may be requested by administrators may be anticipated and addressed in the agreement made with research participants and administrators (Cook, 1976). Because of the tremendous potential for harm from breaches of confidentiality regarding HIV testing, the best procedure for maintaining confidentiality is anonymous testing (Walters, 1988).

Involve the Community in the Design of Interventions

Ignoring community views may prevent the successful implementation of an intervention. The researcher should consider the community's perspective in designing the intervention, as suggested by efforts to design sex education programs (Chethik, 1981). To accomplish this consideration, it is critical to define the relevant communities responsible for youth. Community views may be represented by private or government agencies, legislative bodies, or other appropriate reference groups, as reported in surveys of local attitudes of agency personnel and parents.

Be Explicit Regarding Your Own Biases

Maslow (1969) stated: "The whole scientific process is itself shot through with selectiveness, choice, and preference" (p. 122). Scientists are often unaware of the implicit values underlying their research and their interpretations of others' research. In conducting AIDS research, important values come into conflict, forcing difficult choices (Walters, 1988). Different value systems might lead one researcher to incorporate HIV testing as an essential component of an intervention, while another researcher actively dissuades youth participating in an intervention from being tested. Researchers must try to make their own biases explicit and not rationalize them under the guise of pure empiricism.

Every research project, no matter how brilliantly designed and implemented, is limited in the understanding that it can contribute. Conducting AIDS research with youth is no exception. Therefore, the importance of a study's objectives never justifies ignoring ethical considerations about the research process. To paraphrase Schatzman and Strauss (1973, p. 146), the researcher needs both morality and strategy: the first without the second is ineffectual; the second without the first is cruel.

References

Bayer, R. (1989). Letter. *Journal of the American Medical Association, 261,* 993.

Belcastro, P. A. (1985). Sexual behavior differences between black and white students. *Journal of Sex Research, 21,* 56-67.

Botvin, G. J., Baker, E., Fizazzola, A. D., & Millman, R. B. (1984). Prevention of alcohol misuse through the development of personal and social competence: A pilot study. *Journal of Studies on Alcohol, 45,* 550-552.

Botvin, G. J., Eng., A., & Williams, C. (1980). Preventing the onset of cigarette smoking through life skills training. *Preventive Medicine, 9,* 135-143.

Capron, A. M. (1982). The authority of others to decide about biomedical interventions with incompetents. In W. Gaylin & R. Macklin (Eds.), *Who speaks for the child: The problems of proxy consent.* New York: Plenum.

Carter, W. B., & Deyo, R. A. (1981). The impact of questionnaire research on clinical populations: A dilemma in review of human subjects research resolved by a study of a study. *Clinical Research, 29,* 287-295.

Chethik, B. B. (1981). Developing community support: A first step toward a school sex education program. *Journal of School Health, 51,* 266-270.

Cook, S. W. (1976). Ethical issues in the conduct of research in social relations. In C. Selltiz, L. S. Wrightsman, & S. W. Cook (Eds.), *Research methods in social relations* (3rd ed.; pp. 199-249). New York: Holt, Rinehart & Winston.

Dryfoos, J. (1985). What the United States can learn about prevention of teenage pregnancy from other developed countries. *SIECUS Report, 14,* 1-7.

Elkind, D. (1967). Egocentrism in adolescence. *Child Development, 38,* 1025-1034.

Flora, J. A., & Thoresen, C. E. (1988). Reducing the risk of AIDS in adolescents. *American Psychologist, 43,* 965-970.

Gallup Poll. (1980). *America's families—1980.* Princeton, NJ: The Gallup Organization.

Goldstein, J., Freud, A., & Solnit, A. (1980). *Beyond the best interest of the child.* New York: Free Press.

Greater New York Hospital Association. (1988). *AIDS confidentiality law.* New York: Author.

Gregersen, E. (1986). Human sexuality in cross-cultural perspective. In D. Byrne & K. Kelley (Eds.), *Alternative approaches to the study of sexual behavior* (pp. 87-102). Hillsdale, NJ: Lawrence Erlbaum.

Hayes, C. D. (1987). *Risking the future: Adolescent sexuality, pregnancy, and childbearing*. Washington, DC: National Academy.

Hein, K., Cohen, M. I., Marks, A., Schonberg, S. K., Meyer, M., & McBride, A. (1978). Age at first intercourse among homeless adolescent females. *Journal of Pediatrics, 93*, 147-148.

Jessor, R., Chase, J. A., & Donovan, J. E. (1980). Psychosocial correlates of marijuana use and problem drinking in a national sample of adolescents. *American Journal of Public Health, 70*, 604-613.

Jessor, R., Donovan, J. E., & Widmer, K. (1980). *Psychosocial factors in adolescent alcohol and drug use: The 1978 national sample and the 1974-78 panel study* (Vol. 2). Boulder, CO: University of Colorado, Institute of Behavioral Science.

Kolata, G. (1989, August 4). Strong evidence discovered that AZT holds off AIDS. *New York Times*, pp. A1, B6.

Korcock, M. (1987). Teen's needs different. *U.S. Journal of Drug and Alcohol Dependency, 11*, p

Martin, A. D., & Hetrick, E. S. (1988). The stigmatization of the gay and lesbian adolescent. *Journal of Homosexuality, 15*, 163-183.

Martin, J. L. (1987). The impact of AIDS on gay male sexual behavior patterns in New York City. *American Journal of Public Health, 77*, 578-581.

Marzuk, P., Tierney, H., Tardiff, K., Gross, E. M., Morgan, E. B., Hsu, M., & Mann, J. G. (1988). Increased risk of suicide in persons with AIDS. *Journal of the American Medical Association, 259*, 1332-1333.

Maslow, A. H. (1966). *The psychology of science*. Chicago: Henry Regnery.

New York Statute A.#9765-A (1989).

Office for Protection from Research Risks (OPRR). (1983). *OPRR Reports. Protection of human subjects: Code of federal regulations 45 CFR 46*. Bethesda, MD: Author.

Rotheram-Borus, M. J., Koopman, C., & Bradley, J. (1988, June). *Barriers to successful AIDS prevention programs with runaway youth*. Paper presented at The Georgetown University Child Development Center, Washington, DC.

Schatzman, L., & Strauss, A. L. (1973). *Field research: Strategies for a natural sociology*. Englewood Cliffs, NJ: Prentice-Hall.

Shaffer, D., & Caton, C. L. M. (1984). *Runaway and homeless youth in New York City*. New York: Report to Ittelson Foundation. New York: Ittelson Foundation.

Silber, T. J. (1987). Adolescent marijuana use: The role of the physician. *Adolescence, 22*, 363-370.

Urberg, K., & Robins, R. (1983). *Adolescent invulnerability: Development antecedents, and relationship to risk-taking behavior*. Unpublished manuscript, Wayne State University.

Vener, A. M., & Stewart, C. S. (1974). Adolescent sexual behavior in middle American revisited: 1970-1973. *Journal of Marriage and the Family, 36*, 728-735.

Walters, L. (1988). Ethical issues in the prevention and treatment of HIV infection and AIDS. *Science, 239*, 597-603.

Welbourne-Moglia, A., & Edwards, S. R. (1986). Sex education must be stopped! *SIECUS Report, 15*, 1-3.

Whyte, J. (1987). Letter. *New England Journal of Medicine, 318*, 387.

9

Community Intervention Research on Minors

JOAN E. SIEBER

Community intervention research is applied field research conducted on some group of persons (within their community) who are the recipients of a treatment (intervention) intended to help solve or prevent a problem. The following are examples of community intervention research on minors: (a) A neighborhood clinic provides counseling and methadone to drug-addicted pregnant teenagers; the process and outcomes are studied. (b) An after-school teen social club is organized to teach responsible use of alcohol. Research is conducted on the demography of participants and the resulting leadership skills and change in rate of teen arrests for drinking under the influence. (c) The educational value of "Sesame Street" is tested by providing that program via cable TV to educationally disadvantaged youth in their homes, but not providing "Sesame Street" to matched controls until the experiment is completed. The effects of watching the program for 6 months on educational attainment are then evaluated.

Typically, the persons intervened upon are less powerful than the interveners, and the problem is defined from the perspective of the interveners. Ideally, the research component is designed to provide generalizable knowledge about the intervention. In some cases, however, it is a superficial evaluation designed to justify the continued funding

AUTHOR'S NOTE: I wish to thank Barbara Stanley, Thomas Grisso, Ruth Macklin, and Wendy Bragga for their valuable comments on prior drafts of this chapter. It is much improved because of their assistance.

of the intervention, and the researcher is brought into the intervention after it has been designed. In the latter case, the researcher is likely to be offered inadequate resources to conduct the research properly, may find that the design of the intervention does not permit valid study, and may be given no control over the final editing and dissemination of the results.

As these introductory comments imply, community intervention research on minors may abound with ethical problems above and beyond those that normally occur in applied research on youngsters. This chapter is intended to illustrate (a) how and why community intervention research differs from the more typical research on minors, (b) what ethical issues are likely to arise, and (c) how the investigator may minimize at least those risks that are within his or her purview.

An Introduction to Community Intervention Research and Its Risks

Community intervention research on minors is likely to be initiated because the investigator or other adults in society perceive that a population of young people is at risk. Treatment or prevention activities considered likely to reduce the risk are developed, and research is designed to test the effectiveness of the intervention. Such community interventions are administered sometimes under the auspices of a community institution that is concerned about the welfare of young people (e.g., a school or school district, a community guidance center, a church, the PTA, a recreation center, the Junior League, the Lions Club, the city council, the county court system). Members of one or more community organizations, as well as the researcher, may be involved in administering the intervention and accompanying research. Critical to understanding ethical issues that arise in community intervention research is the role of the researcher vis-à-vis these other community organizations. In some cases, the program is developed primarily by the researcher with the support of relevant community organizations. In other cases, the program is developed primarily by one or more community organizations and the researcher is called in to study and evaluate the process. The ethical issues that may arise in community intervention research depend in part on which of these two roles the researcher occupies.

In community intervention research, the social context of the intervention sometimes makes it difficult to frame the research problem in objective scientific terms. The definition of the research problem may be influenced by false stereotypes about youngsters and their behavior for two reasons. First, community intervention research on minors typically focuses on high-risk behavior that tends to evoke strong, emotionally charged, and often scientifically unsound beliefs among adult members of the community. Second, the intervention typically is initiated by adults who hold and are motivated by just such attitudes. The impetus for the intervention research and the definition of the problem may originate with the funder, with some concerned members of the community, or with the researcher. Unfortunately, none of these parties are necessarily immune to the stereotypes about youngsters that prevail in our culture.

Even if the research problem is *defined* in objective terms, much about the way community intervention research typically operates may stigmatize the youngsters involved. To warrant community intervention, the presenting problem typically is perceived by the community as widespread, serious, and perhaps even scandalous (e.g., child abuse, substance abuse, illiteracy, sexually transmitted diseases, teenage pregnancy, runaways). Thus, merely to identify a youngster as a participant in the research may be stigmatizing. The ethical researcher normally would safeguard confidentiality in every way possible when conducting such sensitive research. However, in community-based research, others may be privy to the data. It is critical, therefore, to ascertain several things in advance: Who will gather the data? Who will have access to them? Who will analyze them? Who will destroy them after they have been analyzed? With what other parties are the data to be shared? How may unique identifiers be made unavailable to any except the principal investigator? Who owns the data? The possibility of gathering anonymous data should not be overlooked. Most intervention research, however, involves at least a pretreatment and posttreatment measurement, meaning that unique identifiers may be gathered with the data.

Even if data are collected anonymously, the very fact of a youngster's physical presence at the research site may give rise to breach of privacy. What young lady would be going into that office where they are interviewing pregnant teenagers, except a young lady who is . . . ? Where the researcher's office is located and who will observe the research participants coming and going from the appointed research site are important considerations. The mere availability of a room beside the principal's office or a cheap rental in a neighborhood store front should not dictate the location of the research site. Again, however, the researcher's power to make these decisions will depend in part on who is in charge of the intervention.

In addition to the difficulty of *defining* the problem objectively is the problem of designing and conducting the research validly. While the community intervention is a field experiment, the conditions under which it is conducted often preclude random assignment of subjects to intervention and control conditions. Moreover, persons do not always receive precisely the treatment and only the treatment to which they were assigned.

Finally, what is done with the results of the study? Who controls what is disseminated and to whom? Much about the nature of young people makes such intervention projects hard to generalize and disseminate validly and ethically. It is difficult for the best of scientific minds to abstract from the intervention setting those elements responsible for the success or failure of the program. It is even more difficult to persuade community members who have dedicated much time and effort to the project, and perhaps draw a salary from it, that no objective evidence exists to justify continuation of the program. It is also difficult to prevent enthusiastic community members from issuing exaggerated and unscientific public statements about the success of the program, especially if such statements will ensure follow-on funding.

As this brief introduction is intended to convey, it is not that no ethical guidelines exist that deal with the problems of intervention research on young people. Rather, the researcher who studies interventions on youngsters is likely to be operating in unusual applied research settings in which "normal" ethical guidelines for research on minors are difficult to apply.

Key Elements to the Difficulties of Intervention Research

Eight terms already have been used that are key to the discussion to follow: *minor, prevention, sensitive research, pretest and posttest, institutions, stereotypes, generalize,* and *dissemination.* Inherent in the definition of each of these terms are elements that make for unusual research settings in which "normal" ethical guidelines are hard to apply.

Minor refers to a child or adolescent. Minors are likely to be selected for participation in a community intervention program because they are engaged in rebellious behavior that their parents do not know about or if they are abused or neglected by their parents. Yet, they may not participate in research without approval of a parent or guardian, except as set forth in 45 C.F.R. 46.408 (DHHS, 1983). This part of the federal regulations governing human research states that it is possible for an IRB to waive the requirement of parental or guardian permission if it is not a reasonable requirement for the protection of the subjects. In place of parental consent, however, must be some appropriate mechanism for protecting children who participate in research. To complicate matters further, a given intervention for young people who are in trouble may include some who are minors and some who are not, presenting a melange of different consent problems.

Minor refers to an age span in which a rapid sequence of psychological, social, and physical growth occurs. Unlike laboratory research in human development, however, community interventions may have practical or political reasons to lump together youngsters who are at very different stages of development. A community intervention program for, say, adolescents may be insensitive to important differences between a 12-year-old and a 19-year-old, or between one 12-year-old and another. Similarly, community interveners may have political reasons to try to "cure" problems that might better be ignored. Some stages of adolescent development may involve extremely disruptive or destructive behavior that quickly ceases when the youngster passes into the next stage of development. Although such behavior (e.g., drunkenness, physical violence) may resemble physically its adult counterpart, it may in fact be psychologically dissimilar and transient.

Prevention refers to an ecological model that seeks to enhance well-being. Prevention seeks to change social systems—to intervene through planned rearrangement of the social ecology in ways that will reduce the incidence of a highly predictable, undesirable consequence. Prevention is measured in populations, not individuals, by measuring the incidence of the undesirable condition before and after implementation of a clearly defined plan of intervention to the identified population (Klein & Goldston, 1977/1980).

Bloom (1979) has defined the range of prevention activities to include (a) educating or otherwise inducing people to apply effective procedures presently known to prevent problems; (b) developing and testing specific prevention hypotheses and then mounting experimental prevention/intervention programs based on that research; and (c) developing and testing nonspecific prevention programs based on the stress model that holds that stressful life experiences may cause accidents, mental or emotional problems, or physical disorders. A risk connected with each of these strategies, especially the latter two, is that the interveners presume to understand the ecology of the lives they seek to influence, and assume that the intervention will cure existing problems and cause no new problems.

Any of these three approaches to prevention with youngsters might involve some intervention in the beliefs and behaviors fostered in the home or community and might expose damaging and illegal parental or child behavior. Another potential risk of prevention interventions is that they identify and work with a group of persons who have a *potential* problem; consequently, such gatekeepers as parents, teachers, and the research participants themselves may create a self-fulfilling prophecy. For example, in the process of administering informed consent, the researcher is likely to describe to the participants the problem they are believed to have and thus may create a stigma that has the power to damage an otherwise undamaged person. Similarly, prevention programs may identify to the rest of the world a problem that really does not exist. Youngsters are particularly vulnerable to stigma because their self-concept is still fluid and rapidly changing and they are also vulnerable to the attitudes and authority of parents and other adults.

Sensitive research refers to research on topics or in contexts where the revelation or use of information gleaned from the research, or the very fact of participation in the research, may stigmatize or otherwise cause psychological, social, legal, or economic damage to the research participants and others. For example, research on the psychological consequences for teenage girls of having an abortion may sensitize subjects to matters that otherwise would not have upset them. Knowledge of a girl's participation would reveal private information about her. Research results indicating that teenagers who have had abortions experience emotional trauma might be used as a basis for denying abortions to girls in the future.

Pretest and posttest or longitudinal research, in which changes within the same person are studied over a considerable period of time, require that data accompanied by unique identifiers be gathered and stored, with identifiers retained at least until the last data collection so that changes within individuals can be analyzed. When the research is on sensitive topics, problems of ensuring confidentiality may become acute.

Institutions likely to foster interventions on young people include a wide range of educational, criminal justice, church, community, and mental health organizations. When interventions are done on minors via such institutions, either the institution arranges for parental consent or serves *in loco parentis*. In either case, the institution is a significant gatekeeper in the process and has its own interests, as well as those of the adolescent, at stake. The institution also may be the sponsor of the research or play a major role in the formulation of the research plan. In any event, it is just one more gatekeeper about which the young person probably has ambivalent feelings, who negotiates the relationship between researcher and youngster.

Stereotypes are oversimplified and biased perceptions. Such adolescent problems as drinking, violence, suicide, getting into trouble with the law, poor school work, and so on, are subject to tremendous stereotyping, distortion, denial, and exaggeration by adults. Youngsters, especially adolescents, fascinate and worry adults because they emulate and mirror qualities of their elders and their culture and they represent the generation that will inherit that culture. Because adults have a major practical and emotional investment in juveniles, such topics as how adolescents learn to use and abuse alcohol, commit crimes, and so on, are hardly neutral ones.

Because these behaviors are learned by teenagers from their adult role models, these behaviors as manifested in teenagers are denied, exaggerated, and scapegoated by adults. Historically in America, this adult reaction has been especially true of adolescent drinking. About every 30 years, a new generation of sincere civic-minded adults rediscovers that adolescents are drinking alcoholic beverages and typically equates use with abuse. Although the turn of the century literature on adolescent drinking is much more naive and unscientific than that of the last decade or two, then, as now, the conclusion typically is that adolescents simply should not drink. Or, as adolescents are told today "Just say no." Although some researchers know better than to define a research problem according to a popular but incorrect stereotype, the funding for research programs is based sometimes on criteria established by popular advocacy groups.

To *generalize* findings is to apply them in seemingly similar other settings. When an intervention program seems to have been successful, communities, rather naturally, expect to generalize them. Because cultural and developmental factors are so diverse among youngsters, however, generalizations drawn from one community study or intervention may not be applicable in other settings. For example, among white adolescent males in the Southeast, the heavy drinker is likely to be a Catholic who attends church more regularly than his nondrinking peer, and who abuses a wide range of toxins (e.g., Sterno) with little knowledge of the consequences. In contrast (and in opposition to commonly held stereotypes) black teenagers of all classes are more likely to drink at home with the family than whites and to drink less frequently and to buy alcoholic beverages less frequently. For black teenagers, church attendance is correlated negatively with drinking (Higgins, Albrecht, & Albrecht, 1977).

Quite apart from the differences between populations of youth and their cultures, interventions themselves differ in unanticipated ways. Because interventions may change many things (some unintentionally), it may be difficult to attribute correctly the cause of observed changes.

Dissemination of research information about intervention in adolescent problems is particularly sensitive both because of problems of generalization and because adults are so nonneutral in their thinking about the problems of youngsters. The dangers of overgeneralization, overkill, scapegoating, or stigmatizing are serious. The researcher may be pressured by community organizers of the intervention to focus on the (real or imagined) successes of the program, rather than give a balanced and objective account. The actual amount of improvement typically produced by interventions is smaller than most people who work within intervention programs want to believe. Even if the researcher reports objectively, project members are likely to try to compensate for this mild account by giving more enthusiastic and exaggerated accounts to the press.

In summary, community intervention on minors typically focuses on a broadly and loosely defined population, not on individuals, and on sensitive problems defined as much by relevant gatekeepers and community members as by the researcher. As such, the usual concept of the autonomous subject and the powerful autonomous researcher and of concern to protect individual subjects from risk may give way naturally to powerful community roles in the research, some form of community consent, and concern for risks to the community. This giving-way is particularly true in cases where parents are not available to give consent, because community consent is not yet a well-developed concept, especially where research on minors is concerned. The following five examples of intervention problems illustrate these issues.

Five Examples of Community Intervention Research on Minors

What do educationally disadvantaged children, adolescent crack users, wards of the court, sexually promiscuous junior high school students, and teen drinkers have in common? Research performed on these five groups of youngsters typically is subject to all of the problems raised above. Five intervention projects are discussed to illustrate these problems: (a) an experiment to determine the effects of "Sesame Street" on various cognitive skills of children, (b) a potential intervention with young crack users, (c) an actual intervention with wards of the court, (d) a project that seeks to help sexually promiscuous youth avoid AIDS, and (e) an especially successful and unusual intervention with teen drinkers, coupled with a discussion of ethical problems that plague research on such interventions.

"Sesame Street" as a Teacher of Cognitive Skills

As the evaluators of various Head Start programs learned, the teachers' aides who were to deliver training to students often failed to teach what they were supposed to teach. Would the television show "Sesame Street," a less personal but more reliable teacher, do a better job of improving the cognitive skills of youngsters? The "Sesame Street" intervention research (Bogartz & Ball, 1971; Cook & Conner, 1976) is an excellent example of a community intervention that was designed to avoid most of the problems that plague researchers and interveners.

"Sesame Street" was provided by cable TV to children in their homes. Matched controls received the cable TV 6 months later in return for their cooperation in the pretesting and posttesting. Parental consent was obtained readily; in fact, even those parents who had little concern for their children's educational attainment welcomed the cable TV as a handy baby-sitter. The testing was strictly under the control of the experimenters and could be carried out anonymously if necessary. Although the educational attainment of youngsters is a sensitive issue, the experiment was not focused on just one neighborhood; the emphasis was on the adequacy of the treatment, not the problems of the youngsters.

The study was not without its problems. In the first year, children were assigned randomly either to viewing or nonviewing conditions. Due to the researchers' lack of control over which children viewed or did not view the show, however, some designated nonviewers became viewers at their own instigation. Consequently, in the next year the researchers selected research sites where the show was available only with a UHF adapter. Another problem was signaled by the lack of gains by some experimental group children. It was determined later that bigger children in their households were controlling the television and not allowing them to watch the "Sesame Street" program.

These problems notwithstanding, the "Sesame Street" intervention research was conducted with notably more scientifically valid and ethically sound procedures than are most community intervention studies. Conner (1982) identified four value premises that underlie arguments favoring the use of a true experimental design in a community intervention.

1. All research clients have a right to status quo activities. Any services normally available should not be denied to anyone. For example, control group members receive their usual services, maintain their regular activities, and are not prevented or discouraged from seeking other available services.
2. All individuals involved in the research are informed about the purposes of the study and the existence of a control group. The existence and necessity for the control group are explained; no deception is attempted at any stage.
3. Equal access to resources and benefits is provided to all. Random selection ensures that each individual has an equal chance of being selected. Participants know that they cannot be certain of the value of the treatment until the research results are obtained. Controls are given access to the desirable treatment after the experiment is over.
4. Scientific utility of the intervention is ensured through proper use of controlled experimentation.

Instrumental to the success of the "Sesame Street" intervention research was a superbly designed study that included the attainment of adequate parental consent and the conduct of the research without the involvement of persons other than the researchers. As we shall see, most community interventions on minors do not enjoy these luxuries.

Crack Users

Crack is one of the most dangerous drugs currently on the street. It is inexpensive and has become the drug of choice among adolescents.

A crack high lasts only about 20 minutes; users come down from their high and must use more of their supply or forage (rob, burglarize) for resources far more frequently than users of other drugs. Crack interferes greatly with normal thought processes. It serves as an aphrodisiac, producing highly promiscuous, indiscriminate sexual behavior. Among some street users, female users barter sex for drugs. The spread of the AIDS virus among crack users has been rapid. Attempts to provide AIDS education have not succeeded with members of this population, who regard AIDS as just another sexually transmitted disease and tend not to consider their future. The incidence of crack use is particularly severe in some inner-city ghettos. The importance of understanding and intervening on crack use is immense, but so are the problems of the research and intervention.

B. Bowser (personal communication, November 1988) and his associates are studying the ecology of crack use in a densely populated, mostly black residential area known for its extremely high incidence of crack use. Data from drug-related street arrests and deaths in the area suggest that a high percentage of drug users are found throughout the neighborhood—which fits the stereotype commonly held by people who have never lived in a ghetto. Interviewing crack users on the street and careful demographic examination of the neighborhood revealed a strikingly different picture. Most of the neighborhood is solidly working and middle class; on most of the streets and in most of the apartment houses there, the neighbors simply would not tolerate drug use. Almost all of the crack users live in a high-rise housing project, and most are unemployed. There, the median age of the residents was found to be 17 years in a census taken a decade ago; the median age is thought to be considerably lower now. The only two places within the neighborhood where crack is bought and used is within the housing project itself and along one block of a street near the project. The implications of this finding for intervention are startlingly different from the standard community intervention ideas that commonly abound. The locus of the intervention needs to be the housing project, which is socially isolated from the rest of the community and which is comprised mostly of young people, an estimated two thirds of whom are minors.

The research that led to this discovery, the research that will inform the intervention, and the intervention itself will involve the researchers in some research activities that differ from ordinary notions of how to do research ethically on minors. The investigators' own childhoods in ghettos provide them with some knowledge of the complexity and diversity of ghetto areas and of the body language and vernacular that makes one acceptable to residents. Among their sponsors is the local black community. Their approach to interviewing addicts is to stop persons in the housing project or on the street who are obviously high on drugs and strike up a conversation. Because the life of the crack user is boring, with only the drug high, sexual encounters, and scrapes with the law to break the monotony, users are happy to talk with an attractive black person who is obviously not of the police and who shows an interest in them. Although many of the persons interviewed come to be known by name to the investigators, the data currently are gathered anonymously. The topic is, obviously, illegal drug use, and the subjects in most cases are minors, though it is not always easy to determine their age. None of the elements of informed consent as defined by federal law would fit appropriately into the conversation between the researcher and the respondents. The interjection of an informed consent statement would typically end the conversation, for the addict wants only to talk about himself or herself and is disinterested in the kinds of "extraneous" information that a proper consent statement would include. Parental consent would be even further out of the question, because many of the respondents do not know the whereabouts of their parents.

Various possible interventions are being considered now. The intervention research is likely to involve HIV testing, longitudinal testing of selected project residents, and attempts at extensive and far-reaching changes in the culture of the project residents. Not the least of the concerns of the researchers is that they may expect to receive death threats from drug dealers whose profits will be threatened by any success of the intervention. The intervention may operate in conjunction with social service agencies, possibly tying the research to other interests and priorities. Because traditional ethical norms of social research do not pertain, what model for responsible stewardship does?

Perhaps community consent coupled with the researchers' own deep concern for the target population are the crucial elements that will foster responsible stewardship and ethical practice. This model seems compatible with Subpart D of 49 FR 9818 (March 8, 1983). The model of community consent, however, needs to be developed and discussed, much as has begun to be done concerning community consent in AIDS research in the gay community, so that researchers will have a clearer idea of how to work effectively with the subjects and how to avoid harm to subjects, members of the community, and themselves (Melton, Levine, Koocher, Rosenthal, & Thompson, 1988). Although the researchers will need to work closely with community members and organizations, they will need to retain as their prerogative the control of confidentiality, data, and dissemination.

Remembering the simple elegance of the "Sesame Street" intervention, the reader may ask, "But why not also retain control of the intervention, itself?" The answer is that it may not be within the power of the researchers to control the intervention. Unlike the "Sesame Street" researchers, these researchers face a complex and difficult problem of gaining access to their research subjects. Their access to and relationship with the subjects depends critically on their establishment of relationships with community gatekeepers who have the power to facilitate or prevent the research. It is those gatekeepers who have credibility and political power in their neighborhood, who can persuade the potential subjects to participate, and who may be able to marshall some assistance in protecting the project from drug lords whose well-being is threatened by the project. Aspects of the project, such as drug dealing among the gatekeepers themselves, may not please an IRB that oversees the research. That problem, however, is not within the control of the researcher, and it should not stand in the way of the research.

Wards of the Court

Children who are wards of the court are increasingly an appropriate population for applied social research and community intervention. In most cases, the court or a specific judge is likely to serve as guardian and overseer, but this service does not necessarily reduce the diversity of input from other sectors of the community or reduce the kinds of problems described above, as illustrated by the research of Blackman and diSibio (in preparation).

This study of the impact of a court-appointed special advocate on the self-esteem of juvenile court dependents had two purposes: (a) to investigate self-esteem, locus of control, and depression in children who are court dependents; and (b) to examine the effects of a volunteer child advocate program that was designed to assist children through the legal process. The goals of the study were to determine the needs of dependent children, to determine whether advocates help to meet those needs, and to make recommendations about ways to

improve the children's emotional well-being. The study was conducted under the sponsorship of the juvenile court in two counties and
in cooperation with various agencies concerned about juvenile court
dependents. Unlike the planned intervention with IV drug users, this
study was largely under the control of the researchers, but that did not
make it entirely controllable.

The intervention group consisted of 180 children aged 8 to 18 who
were juvenile court dependents. Part of the sample was referred from the
Court Designated Child Advocate (CDCA) program in one county. The
remainder of the sample was referred by the newly created advocate program in the other county. Control subjects were obtained from other
nearby counties that referred children who would have been assigned to
a child advocate program if that county had one.

All children were administered three tests: the Nowicki-Strickland
Locus of Control Scale, the Children's Depression Inventory, and the
Piers-Harris Children's Self-Concept Scale, all of which are self-rating
scales requiring children to respond by circling the answer that best
corresponds to their feelings. The logistics of testing proved complex,
and the researchers were persuaded by the CDCA program personnel
that the tests be administered individually or in small groups, with
small-group administration being preferred whenever feasible. The
testing was proctored by volunteers from the CDCA program, selected Junior League volunteers, and members of the research team.
A test proctor gave standard instructions and reminded children not to
write their names on the test protocols.

Consent proved to be a troublesome process for the investigators
both because of one of the judges and because of the difficulty of determining who was an actual subject and who was not.

One of the judges who issued the court order that the study be done
was unwilling to write a separate letter of consent or sign a consent form
for each subject, arguing that he was too busy and that the court order
was tantamount to his consent. The investigator and the IRB had to turn
to a lawyer and ex-judge to validate the accuracy of that claim.

Next came the problem of determining who really was a subject
and who was not. Most of the testing settings that the CDCA personnel wished to set up were located where many young people pass.
Wards of the court tend to be shuttled from place to place, and youngsters who happened to be located temporarily at a given testing site
were likely to be included in the testing even though they were not
among those for whom consent had been given.

The problems of risk also proved difficult. The subjects were vulnerable youngsters who had experienced abuse and disappointment much of their lives. The questions they would answer were ones likely to evoke recollections of past pain and sorrow and feelings of hopelessness. To the extent that the budding psychologists who administered the tests established rapport and a sympathetic relationship, the subjects might feel that they could reach out for help. What if the researcher then efficiently packed up the tests and took off without so much as an individual conversation with such a subject? What should the researcher look for as symptoms of deep concern and reaching out? How should proctors be trained? How much help should or could the researcher provide in response to such help-seeking? Would tracking of those who needed help be possible in the weeks and months to come? The difficulty of giving instructions and detecting and responding to expressions of need was compounded by the wide age range of these youngsters and the tremendous range of presenting problems.

The problems of internal and external validity were also troubling in this one-shot testing of youngsters at all stages of development. For purposes of learning the long-term effects of advocacy, it would be useful to be able to follow youngsters through at least several weeks of association with the program and to gather extensive background information on each, but that would entail gathering identifiable data and tracking the movement of people who are moved about a great deal. The control group could not, for practical reasons, be adequately matched, because they necessarily had to come from a county that did not have a CDCA program. How should such difficult-to-interpret findings be communicated to the sponsors and others?

The judges who decreed this study were, in essence, the community representatives who provided consent and oversight. They exemplify one of the problems with the concept of community consent: One judge is a man who has always cared deeply about the problems of juvenile wards of the court and who visited the project frequently. The other judge had little time or interest to invest in the project.

Sexually Promiscuous Junior High School Students

Perhaps one of the most vexing problems of research and intervention is that of preventing teen pregnancy and the spread of AIDS. It seems obvious to some that the solution is for parents to educate their children in these matters and for youngsters to learn to make decisions that are in their own self-interest. Sex educators who have worked with parents and schools have learned that (a) many parents know very little about sex and disease and do not wish to let their ignorance be known by seeking education; (b) in patriarchal families it is the practice to try to control the sexuality of females by stern prohibition, which is highly unsuccessful; (c) many youngsters do not readily understand that they can exercise intelligent choice in these matters and do not have the factual background to do so; (d) parents who lack knowledge about sexuality usually will not consent to letting their children receive sex education, and violently oppose having their children be given information about birth control and disease control; and (e) most school administrators routinely forbid research or intervention in this area because of the problems this creates with parents. In matters of sex, as with drinking, youngsters are to "Just say no." Worse, many parents believe that "If you talk about it, you'll do it."

The design of intervention research involving an education that teaches youngsters about sexuality, AIDS, and disease prevention depends on solving the problem of parental consent. In one case, this dependence meant finding an education and consent structure that was already in place and supported by the community. Several school districts have created health clinics within each school where students may register (with their parents' consent) in courses having to do with health care. Part of the registration and parental consent procedure is to provide prospective students and their parents with an outline of the topics to be included in a given course and the activities that will be included, including research evaluating the program. This project will seek to provide the resources to enrich these existing educational settings, in return for which the research may be allowed.

This project has not yet been funded or begun. It is safe to predict, however, that the gatekeepers (the school administration and the parents) will have considerable control over what is done. Integral to the success of this program, if indeed it gets underway, will be the fully informed consent of parents, the confidentiality of test results, and the discretion with which the findings are reported, focusing on the adequacy of the treatment, not the problems of those who are being educated.

Adolescent Drinking

Adolescent drinking is a topic around which community concern and community intervention have existed for many decades. Hence, it provides an opportunity to summarize the perennial hazards of community intervention research on adolescent drinking, as well as problems connected with a specific project.

The popular view of adolescent drinking is that it simply should not occur, despite the fact that it is an adult behavior and teenagers emulate adults. Hence, a massive national campaign has been created in which adolescents are told "Just say no." The student of human development and social learning readily senses that something is wrong with this idea. The learning of appropriate, problem-free patterns of adult drinking is the result of complex learning over the years of childhood and adolescence. Likewise, the learning of comfortable and satisfying patterns of abstinent behavior is based on a complex set of beliefs and behaviors requiring extensive prior learning. Driver education movies that show wrecked cars and dead teenagers, and adults who say "Do as I say, not as I do," do not fulfill scientific requirements for an effective alcohol use or abstinence-learning program for adolescents.

Because American society is once again putting considerable political energy and federal funds into intervention programs to combat an allegedly new epidemic of teenage alcohol abuse, now is an appropriate time to examine the nature of adolescent drinking, the definition of what is to be intervened upon, the kinds of interventions that seem to work, and problems of evaluating such interventions.

Adolescent alcohol use and abuse is a complex topic—far more complex than adult stereotypes about "adolescent drinking" would suggest. We have discussed already the difficulty of defining *adolescent* or *minor*. In addition, each of the words *adolescent, alcohol, use,* and *abuse* refers to a complex concept and also contributes to the difficulty of framing the problem objectively and generalizing the results responsibly.

Alcohol refers to various beverages categorized as beer, wine, and spirits. Most research on adolescent drinking does not take beverage specificity into consideration, but research that does so indicates that adolescent drinking behavior is highly beverage specific. Moreover, the behavior of adult role models is also highly beverage specific. Research consistently shows that beer is the beverage of choice of adolescents and young adults. In adolescence, the ratio of beer drinking to wine and liquor drinking is typically at least 2 to 1 for boys and girls, except that in some locations girls drink more wine than boys (Wechsler, 1979). Beer is the preferred drink of men and young adults, with older drinkers and women showing a preference for wine and spirits. The behavioral implications of these differences in beverage preference are dramatic. For example, Berger and Snortum (1985) found that those who prefer beer typically drink to higher levels of intoxication, are more likely to drive after drinking, and tend to consider driving while intoxicated to be less serious. These findings generalize across age, sex, education, income, and marital status. Thus, although beer has the lowest concentration of alcohol, it is actually not a drink of moderation. Beer advertisements target the youth market, however, and special concessions exist for the legal purchasing age and advertising of beer.

Use of alcohol can refer to any of a diverse set of uses. It could refer to the Jewish youngster who drinks wine with his family regularly; Jews have a low rate of per capita consumption and a low rate of alcohol-related problems, although most are drinkers and have been wine drinkers since childhood. It could refer to the girl whose parents insist that she drink whiskey with them when they are on an alcoholic binge and who may be haunted by alcohol-related problems all her life. It could refer to the young woman whose parents invite and permit her to join adult guests in having a cocktail at parties given at home and who learns responsible drinking behavior. It could refer to the teenager who drinks beer in cars because he is not allowed to drink at home and who outgrows this form of rebellion in a few years, but not before getting into trouble with the law.

Each of these cases depicts a different meaning of *alcohol use*. To put this point more technically, the meaning of *alcohol use* depends on (a) quantity, (b) frequency, (c) weight of user, (d) duration of drinking episode, (e) user's experience, (f) context of use, (g) psychological and physiological status of the user, (h) the way the role of the drinker is defined, (i) the way the act of drinking is defined, and (j) patterns of alcohol use over time (Bacon, 1976). Because of the difficulty of employing an adequate operational definition of *drinking* (abusive or otherwise), the literature abounds with inconsistent definitions. Bacon notes that two major studies of adolescents (each having over 10,000 subjects) defined *drinking* as having more than one sip a year, and drinking at least 5 days out of every week, respectively. Apart from such oversimplification and inconsistency, no research could feasibly employ all 10 of the factors in its definition of alcohol use, despite the importance of those distinctions.

Consequently, adolescent problem drinking tends to be defined as drunkenness, especially when it involves trouble with family, teachers, police, or friends, or drunken driving. Defined in this way, adolescent problem drinking is often a transitory testing of limits set by the adult world, which soon gives way to moderate and responsible drinking. This concept of problem drinking does not imply an entity such as alcoholism or any kind of pathology (Cahalan, 1970; Donovan & Jessor, 1978; Jessor & Jessor, 1977), but only that other problems arise in association with the drinking.

Problems of defining what is to be intervened upon naturally follow from these problems of defining adolescent problem drinking. The literature on adolescent drinking abounds with warnings that drinking leads to such things as getting pregnant, dropping out of school, getting poor grades, using drugs, engaging in burglaries, and so forth. These warnings cause society to focus on alcohol as the root cause of antisocial behavior and to ignore the more complex psychosocial factors that appear to underlie both drinking and the other problems associated with it.

As Doris (1982) and Davies (1930) document, social scientists and community members made a similar error at the turn of the century with respect to mental retardation, which they warned was the cause of prostitution, delinquency, alcoholism, and vagrancy. They warned policymakers that unless the retarded were prevented from reproducing, these problems would be multiplied, threatening the extinction of Western civilization.

False stereotypes about teenage drinking, some of which are held even by funding agencies, make it difficult for interveners to approach this problem objectively. Some false stereotypes are as follows:

1. *Teenage drinking involves guzzling and carousing.* In fact, research indicates that most teenage drinking occurs at home with parents or at parties in the homes of friends (Milgram, 1982).
2. *Teenage drinking is on the increase.* In fact, empirical research shows that a dramatic increase in adolescent drinking occurred throughout the Western world between 1940 and 1965, but since 1965 has leveled off (Zucker & Harford, 1983).
3. *Drinking is more prevalent among minorities, children from the wrong side of the tracks, and those who are socially maladjusted.* In fact, adolescent drinking is more prevalent among whites than blacks or other minorities, highly prevalent among white middle and upper-middle-class teens, and bears no relationship to whether the youngster is a member of

student organizations, participates in scholastic athletics, holds office in organizations, or comes from a broken home (Forney, 1984).

4. *Teenage drinking is an American and Western problem.* In fact, the greatest threat of alcohol problems in adolescence is found in areas of the world undergoing rapid sociocultural and economic change, such as Africa and Latin America, and especially among primitive peoples in settings where formerly effective sociocultural controls on overindulgence have broken down and alcohol has become more prevalent. Patterns of drinking in European countries and the United States are highly similar.

5. *Advertising and the peer culture lure teenagers to drink against their parents' wishes.* In fact, advertising does not noticeably affect adolescent drinking (Smart, 1979), and the tendency is for teenagers to respect their parents' wishes. The children of abstaining parents typically are abstainers. Although peer group participation may expose teenagers to models of behavior other than those of their parents, adolescent cliques tend to form around similarity of life-style of the members' families. Young people do not invent ideas about drinking or abstinence, but learn them in the process of being socialized. Teenagers do differ from adults in their attitudes toward alcoholism, but they differ in the direction of being more moralistic and blaming (Lorch & Hughes, 1986).

How do these false stereotypes arise? Perhaps one of the most interesting questions in this connection is what motivates adults to create and maintain misconceptions about adolescent drinking that probably harm rather than benefit teenagers. Negative and repressive approaches to socializing adolescents with regard to alcohol are unlikely to produce responsible alcohol use or a healthy basis for abstinence. What models of socialization will prevail in the next decade? A new style temperance movement is gaining momentum in American society. What kinds of research and interventions will it foster?

Intervening on Adolescent Abuse of Alcohol

The most prevalent interventions are school-related programs that are, essentially, modern "health education" courses. Typically, these advocate abstinence and are driven by belief in many of the erroneous stereotypes listed above.

Less prevalent but far more promising are the community intervention programs that accept teen drinking as likely and offer education, training, and community services that enable teenagers to drink responsibly when they do drink. The most impressive of these programs is Friday Night Live, an intervention program that does not operate at all according to traditional ethical tenets of human research on minors. In fact, it rather more resembles the kind of intervention that Bowser and others hope to establish to combat crack use in housing projects. It largely circumvents consent of parents, involves a far-reaching level of community organization and intervention, and focuses on study of population statistics rather than individual cases.

Friday Night Live, a multimedia assembly program on drinking and driving, was begun in Washington State by Paul Wyatt. Wyatt recognized that student activity needed to be coupled with the assembly, so he teamed up with Students Against Drunk Driving (SADD). Friday Night Live moved to Sacramento County, California, where the program was shown at high school assemblies to establish 40 SADD chapters and then provided them with leadership training and other activities and resources.

A Friday Night Live assembly is a very high-energy event. Perhaps 2,000 students are present and are greeted with their favorite loud rock music and a three slide-projector, fast-moving presentation, starting with slides taken at their own school. Then comes a party scene. A girl drives off under the influence of alcohol. She is arrested and the actual arrest scene is depicted in some detail.

The audience typically is quite hushed by this time. Then the slide show stops and a girl takes over and tells the audience the story of how she lost her eye because she let her boyfriend drive drunk. She tells how it has affected her life to have just one eye. The audience then gets to hear from a student whose best friend was killed in a drunk-driving accident. The concluding message is "Don't party with alcohol. But if you do, be responsible for that decision." At the conclusion of the assembly, students are given a chance to join a SADD chapter.

Friday Night Live keeps in touch with each of its 40 chapters with activities and promotional materials. It provides leadership training, helps chapters set goals, and encourages chapters to share problems and problem-solving strategies. Dances, prizes, special events with legislators, community awareness programs, and help-your-friends programs are given. A leadership conference is provided in which students learn public-speaking skills, uses of the media, decision strategies, and goal-setting techniques.

A safe-driving program has been developed, drawing the top students from each of the 40 chapters. A group of 125 students is now trained and qualified to give free, safe, confidential rides home to students who have been drinking or whose driver has been drinking. Students answer the hotline from 10 p.m. to 2 a.m. Friday and Saturday nights. Thus, teenagers whose parents would not respond to their plea for a no-fault ride home can call on this organization for confidential service. So far, over 800 rides home have been provided in little over a year.

The result? According to Sharon Dais, Special Projects Coordinator for Friday Night Live, in 18 months, teen DUI deaths and injuries in Sacramento County have been reduced by 36% (S. Dais, personal communications, 1987)! Note that these hard data on teen DUI deaths and injuries were obtained from government records. This program does not count as human research. It does not require parental consent, IRB review, or any of the other ethical requirements of human research.

Problems of Evaluating Such Intervention

This unusually effective intervention has been possible partly because it was not conceived as a research program and did not seek to measure individual behavior. A complex and uncontrolled array of activities are involved. Students do not need parental consent to participate because it is not research, and many students may do things connected with the program that are against their parents' wishes. The merits of the program, in terms of individual change, warrant study and probably will be studied someday soon. When that occurs, all of the problems discussed in the introduction of this chapter probably will pertain.

Many scientific and ethical problems are connected with community interventions such as Friday Night Live, however, with or without emphasis on study of the individual.

1. Program directors and staff typically are true believers in their program's success and work with great dedication, conveying the importance of the program to their young charges. Moreover, the apparent success of a program is likely to mean continuation of its funding and the employment of its staff. Thus, two effects are likely to be (a) the Hawthorne Effect, a boost in morale and productivity that comes from receiving

special attention; and (b) the "finagle factor," the handling of experiments so that the most positive possible results are obtained with or without resorting to downright fraud.

2. Multiple approaches within programs and concatenations of school, community, media, and other programs are more successful than singular approaches. Thus, the success of any component tells little without information on what else is occurring. A program planted in a community where other programs are starting up is likely to show greater success than otherwise.

3. Programs must be based on the perceived needs and willing efforts of volunteer members of the community in which they are based. This team-building effort is vital to the success of the program. This element often conflicts, however, with the need to do valid research, especially with the need to control conditions and to respect individual privacy and preserve confidentiality of data.

4. The charisma, energy, and intelligence of the local leaders are necessary but not sufficient ingredients for achieving success in a given setting. How are these ingredients described and taken into account in research, dissemination, and generalization of the findings?

5. The external validity of a program—that is, the effectiveness of the program in new setting B, given that it was successful in setting A—cannot be guaranteed. Hence, researchers should look for robustness of good results. Do they occur in many settings? Although evaluation of specific programs is of some interest, the main concern should be to discover which general strategies tend to work and why. Probably no single project can hope to contribute more than a small part of that knowledge, but may claim otherwise.

6. The kinds of outcomes that are most measurable often also are manipulated most easily by people who wish to make the program look good. Teachers can teach especially to those specific skills that will be measured, as in the New York Regents Exam. Similarly, police can alter their reporting practices to show improvements that they are "sure" are occurring anyhow.

7. Rigorous evaluation is extremely difficult and costly. Unless the funding source is truly eager for evaluation and willing to allocate a substantial portion of the program budget to evaluation, adequate evaluation will not occur. Politicians, community leaders, and program developers have little incentive to seek rigorous evaluation. Such evaluation typically reveals far less program success than the program staff, clientele, or community think is occurring. Even when adequate evaluation does occur, the project may find reasons not to report it, or the final report of the

evaluation may receive a heavy "final editing" by the project director because the findings are so disappointing.

8. Programs usually claim to have an evaluation component, but typically that does not mean research. It means that the staff and others sat down and decided what they had accomplished and what they should do next.

9. Programs are more (as well as less) than what they measure. Many valuable outcomes can be communicated only by anecdote. Much happens after the evaluation team has packed up and moved to a new project. Changing people and organizations is not a quick and linear process. Typically, the first few years are needed to learn how to run the program effectively and to persuade people that things can be done differently. Later, the change comes to be a self-fulfilling prophecy, and by that time no one is impressed. Also, by then, the program has evolved far past its original form.

Summary

Research on community interventions with youngsters is likely to be a study performed on a hodge-podge of youngsters to determine the effects of a highly uncontrolled set of events. Issues of consent of participants or their parents, validity of the research, generalizability of findings, adequacy of controls, qualifications of all of the people who are conducting the intervention and evaluation, concern for risk to individuals and compensation for harm, distributive justice with respect to which youngster receives which benefits and inconveniences, and appropriateness of the recruitment procedures are all likely to be ignored, and perhaps they must be, in some cases. But in the absence of clear ethical norms and legal safeguards, how should the model of community collaboration and/or consent be guided, and what elements should that model contain?

Some community intervention with minors has many elements in common with field research done by anthropologists, especially in primitive cultures. The researcher is not the most powerful agent in the setting; much of what can be done must be done with the advice, consent, and assistance of powerful members of the larger community. Individual autonomy on the part of the researcher and subject is barely present. The risks and benefits of the research may redound as much to the community as to the youngsters intervened upon. The data of greatest interest may be population data, not individual data.

Individual data and unique identifiers may not be gathered; hence, confidentiality and privacy may pertain more to the community than to the individuals within it. Risk and harm may be more likely to be political, economic, or social consequences to the community than harm to an individual.

Yet, it is individual youngsters whose lives are intervened upon. Can guidelines for responsible stewardship by researchers, supporting communities, and IRBs be articulated? If so, how can they be applied and enforced in such far-flung, changing and complex settings? Or can they be?

References

Bacon, S. (1976). Defining adolescent alcohol use: Implications for a definition of adolescent alcoholism. *Journal of Studies on Alcohol, 37,* 1014-1019.

Berger, D. E., & Snortum, J. R. (1985). Alcoholic beverage preferences of drinking driving violators. *Journal of Studies on Alcohol, 46*(3), 232-239.

Blackman, D. C., & diSibio, M. P. *Volunteer advocates in the court system: Do the children benefit?* (Manuscript in preparation)

Bloom, B. L. (1979). Prevention of mental disorders: Recent advances in theory and practice. *Community Mental Health Journal, 15,* 179-191.

Bogartz, G. A., & Ball, S. (1971). *The second year of Sesame Street: A continuing evaluation* (Vols. 1 and 2). Princeton, NJ: Educational Testing Service.

Cahalan, D. (1970). *Problem drinkers: A national survey.* San Francisco: Jossey-Bass.

Conner, R. F. (1982). Random assignment of clients in social experimentation. In J. E. Sieber (Ed.), *The ethics of social research: Surveys and experiments* (Vol. 1; pp 57-77). New York: Springer-Verlag.

Cook, T. D., & Conner, R. F. (1976). Sesame Street around the world: The educational impact. *Journal of Communications, 26,* 155-164.

Davies, S. P. (1930). *Social control of the mentally deficient.* New York: Thomas Y. Crowell.

Department of Health and Human Services (DHHS). (1983). *Protection of human subjects code of federal regulations* 45 CFR 46. Washington, DC: Government Printing Office.

Donovan, J. E., & Jessor, R. (1978). Adolescent problem drinking: Psychosocial correlates in a national sample study. *Journal of Studies on Alcohol, 39*(9), 1506-1524.

Doris, J. (1982). Social science and advocacy. *American Behavioral Scientist, 26*(2), 199-234.

Forney, M. (1984). A discriminant analysis of adolescent problem drinking. *Journal of Drug Education, 14*(4), 347-355.

49 FR 9818 (March 8, 1983).

Higgins, P. C., Albrecht, G. L., & Albrecht, M. H. (1977). Black-white adolescent drinking: The myth and the reality. *Social Problems, 25*(2), 215-224.

Jessor, R., & Jessor, S. L. (1977). *Problem behavior and psychosocial development: A longitudinal study of youth.* New York: Academic Press.

Klein, D. C., & Goldston, S. E. (1977/1980). *Primary prevention: An idea whose time has come* (Proceedings of a pilot conference on primary prevention, April 2-4, 1976; DHHS Publication No. ADM 80-447). Washington, DC: Department of Health and Human Services.

Lorch, B. D., & Hughes, R. H. (1986). Youths' perceptions of alcoholism. *Journal of Alcohol and Drug Education, 31,* 54-63.

Melton, G. B., Levine, R. J., Koocher, G. P., Rosenthal, R., & Thompson, W. C. (1988). Community consultation in socially sensitive research: Lessons from clinical trials of treatments for AIDS. *American Psychologist, 43*(7), 575-581.

Milgram, G. G. (1982). Youthful drinking: Past and present. *Journal of Drug Education, 12*(4) 289-308.

Smart, R. G. (1979). Priorities in minimizing alcohol problems among young people. In H. T. Blane & M. E. Chafetz (Eds.), *Youth, alcohol, and social policy* (pp. 229-261). New York: Plenum.

Wechsler, H. (1979). Patterns of alcohol consumption among the young: High school, college, and general populations studies. In H. T. Blane & M. E. Chafetz (Eds.), *Youth, alcohol and social policy* (pp. 39-58). New York: Plenum.

Zucker, R. A., & Harford, T. C. (1983). National study of the demography of adolescent drinking practices in 1980. *Journal of Studies on Alcohol, 4*(6), 974-985.

Epilogue

BARBARA STANLEY
JOAN E. SIEBER

The task force on research on minors sought to identify key issues that are important to consider when planning and conducting research on children and adolescents. The following issues emerged:

- waiver of parental permission for research participation
- implications of the concept of "mature minor" for the conduct of research on minors
- evaluating risk in relation to the psychological development of research participants
- special circumstances of research on minors, especially ethnographic research and community intervention
- assent process considerations, including forms, pilot studies to determine youngsters' capacity to understand, and presentation of the process to youngsters.

As the preceding chapters abundantly demonstrate, these issues are complex. None of them yield to simple rules. Every decision must be conditioned on relevant psychological, legal, scientific, and situational factors. Accordingly, we offer a summary of these issues with the following three caveats:

1. This summary may not be very useful to those who have not read the preceding chapters.

2. Nothing in this summary is to be construed as a definitive resolution of the issue.
3. This summary is not a substitute for good professional judgments, knowledge of one's research population and setting, knowledge of the laws governing human research, and professional consultation.

Waiver of Parental Permission

Department of Health and Human Services regulation 46.408(c) (see Appendix in chapter 2) provides, under certain circumstances, that minors may participate in research based on their own consent in the absence of permission of a parent or guardian. Care must be taken in interpreting this regulation.

Parents' incompetence is unlikely to represent an adequate reason by itself for waiving the general requirement. Children of legally incompetent parents have guardians whose consent may be sought. When parents' deficiencies are insufficient to have resulted in appointment of guardians, their deficiencies probably do not constitute grounds for abrogating their right to decide whether their children may participate in research.

Parental absence or unavailability may be grounds for waiving parental consent, provided the research objectives are important and proper steps have been taken to protect the research participants. A variety of circumstances exist under which it may be impossible or impractical to contact the parents. For example, street children who are drug dealers may or may not have available parents or guardians, but in any case, the potential research participants probably would make it impossible for the researcher to make or act upon this determination.

Abusive or neglectful parents obviously cannot be counted on to act in their children's best interests. *Parents who are in an adversarial stance vis-à-vis their children* present a more complex problem; typically, they are feeling angry and punitive because of their youngster's misbehavior (see chapter 6). Waiver of parental consent may be appropriate under these conditions when the children are being treated for abuse or neglect, are identified legally as incorrigible or delinquent, or are in the custody of a hospital or other institution.

The "Mature Minor"

The meaning of "mature minor" is important because under certain circumstances being a mature minor is viewed as sufficient condition to waive parental permission. Much controversy surrounds this standard as a basis for waiving parental permission, however. The mere fact that parental permission would be superfluous for certain "mature minors" does not by itself make parental permission an unreasonable requirement. Minors may have a constitutional right to participate in some research without parental consent, however; hence, state law may not prohibit such participation. Some theorize that the right of privacy that entitles mature minors to obtain abortions without parental knowledge or permission should also entitle them to consent to research. No court has ruled on this claim.

This matter is further complicated by the lack of any clear legal definition of "mature minor." Court rulings offer some guidance:

1. The determination of maturity must be made on a case-by-case basis, rather than by category. For example, a state may not simply define all 17-year-olds as mature for purposes of exercising the constitutional right to abortion.
2. The mature minor need not be economically independent of the parents, or even emotionally or intellectually mature in all respects. In *Bellotti v. Baird* (1979), which considered an abortion decision, the court found that "the fact that a minor may be very much an adult in some respects does not mean that his need and opportunity for growth under parental guidance and discipline have ended."
3. The minor should be "mature enough and well enough informed to make her abortion decision, in consultation with her physician, independently of her parents' wishes."

Statutes vary from state to state regarding the kind of treatment minors may obtain without parental consent. Some of these statutes might be construed to encompass authority for minors to consent to participate in some research; state law is silent, however, on the subject of participation of minors in research. This silence is less of a barrier than if state law explicitly prohibited such participation.

Evaluating Risk

Attempts to evaluate research risk for children and adolescents must take developmental factors into consideration. Children are special as a research population because of (a) limitations in their capacity to give informed consent; (b) their cognitive and psychological immaturity; (c) constraints on their self-determination and independent decision making; (d) their unequal power vis-à-vis social authorities (including parents and teachers who often provide proxy consent, as well as researchers); (e) their limited range of prior experiences in research settings; (f) the unique configuration of child, parental, and state interests relating to their research participation; and because (g) in nonclinical, social research they are seldom the direct beneficiaries of research participation. For these reasons, the following should guide the evaluation of research risk:

A developmental orientation should frame the judgments of risk. Within this orientation, children at younger ages may be *more vulnerable* to certain aspects of research participation when compared with older children, they may be *less vulnerable* than older children with respect to other risks, and for still other risks essentially *no differences* may exist between younger and older children with respect to vulnerability. In other words, judgment of risk within a developmental framework means that different domains of risk must be appraised independently. Simple, linear developmental models of risk vulnerability are inappropriate.

Graded rather than threshold judgments of risk should be made. In many respects, researchers are well suited to perform graded evaluations of research risk because their knowledge of developmental processes enables them to appraise more acutely how children of different ages are likely to be affected by research procedures.

Focus on risk, not benefit, in maintaining standards of decent treatment of minors in research. Benefit estimation involves prediction of unknowns; research risks are more knowable and have a greater direct influence on the research participation.

Consider any special characteristics of the research population. For example, the background or environment of maltreated children or incarcerated adolescents may make them vulnerable to risks that would not arise for other youngsters; likewise, special benefits may accrue to their research participation that would not occur for other populations of youngsters.

Special Circumstances of Research on Minors

Ethnographic research raises problems of consent or permission. The criteria for deciding who needs to give permission or consent are (a) the organizational norms within the institution being studied or observed, and (b) whether the setting is public or private; public behavior generally may be observed without consent.

Community intervention poses special problems of confidentiality. A community intervention may be a much more open or public operation than most standard research projects. Concerns about confidentiality as it pertains to data gathering and dissemination of findings are important to consider. The actual intervention may be under separate control from the research that evaluates it. Problems can arise with data falling into the hands of other groups indirectly involved in the intervention (e.g., law enforcement, school authorities, civic groups, or media representatives).

Community norms dictate the appropriateness of any intervention. It is critical to define the relevant communities in order to decide what is an ethical and culturally sensitive intervention approach.

Assent Process Considerations

Plan consent forms. Research involving high risk populations must anticipate the necessity of disclosing certain of those behaviors to parents or other authorities. Youngsters must be informed of the specific behaviors that need to be disclosed for the best possible care to be provided to the youngsters. The kinds of high-risk behaviors that need to be anticipated vary with the setting, the population, their age, and whether parental guidance is available. Sexual abuse must always be reported, whereas drinking alcohol is unlikely to be considered serious unless the youngster is quite young and the drinking excessive. Youngsters who are sexually active or who are injection drug users are likely to be at higher risk than youngsters who do not engage in these behaviors.

Pilot studies should be conducted to determine youngsters' capacity to understand and give assent.

The consent materials presented to youngsters should be modified to take into account their ability level. Modifications might include the use of illustrations, larger print, spoken or written language matched to the child's level of understanding, grouping of information with titles as key words, presentation of the information in a non-threatening environment, allowing the child and parent to take information home, matching the speed of presentation to the child's level of processing, and repeated presentation after assessment to determine level of understanding. The assimilation of the information by the child may be modified, using correction for mistakes, prompting, and reinforcement for understanding.

****

Legal and ethical principles governing research on children and adolescents are forged through experience. No researcher, ethicist, government official, or lawyer can foresee all of the problems that will become topics of research. They cannot foresee the confluence of forces that cause society to reappraise the priorities that should govern research. This book represents current perceptions of how to resolve ethical dilemmas in research on children and adolescents. These ideas will change as society changes.

References

Bellotti v. Baird, 443 U.S. 622 (1979).

Department of Health and Human Services (DHHS). (1983). *Protection of human subjects code of federal regulations* 45 CFR 46. Washington, DC: Government Printing Office.

Author Index

Aber, J. L., 51, 62
Albrecht, G. L., 169, 186
Albrecht, M. H., 169, 186
Altman, I., 64, 87
American Psychological Association, 34, 58, 62, 77, 85, 105
Anderson, B. F., 58, 63
Annas, G., 129, 139
Appelbaum, P. S., 78, 85
Areen, J., 4
Arkes, H. R., 58, 60

Bacon, S., 179, 186
Baker, E., 154, 160
Ball, S., 170, 186
Barrett, K. C., 47, 62
Bartolome, W. G., 53, 62
Baumrind, D., 39, 62
Bayer, R., 149, 160
Beauchamp, T. L., 63
Belcastro, P. A., 156, 160
Berger, D. E., 178, 186
Berman, J. J., 78, 86
Blackman, D. C., 174, 186
Blane, H. T., 187
Bloom, B. L., 166

Bluestein, J., 105
Bogartz, G. A., 170, 186
Boruch, R. F., 81, 85
Botvin, G. J., 154, 160
Bowser, B., 172
Bradley, J., 156, 161
Brandeis, L., 67, 87
Brennan, M., 33, 62
Brouwer, R., 138, 139
Brown, P. G., 104, 105
Bush, M., 74, 85
Byrne, D., 161

Cahalan, D., 180, 186
Cain, K. M., 44, 62
Campbell, S., 135, 138, 139
Campos, J. J., 47, 62
Capron, A. M., 129, 131, 147, 160
Carter, W. B., 158, 160
Caton, C. L. M., 148, 161
Cecil, J. S., 81, 85
Chafetz, M. E., 187
Chase, J. A., 154, 161
Chethik, B. B., 159, 160
Cicchetti, D., 51, 62
Cohen, M. I., 161

194

Subject Index

About the Authors

Judith Areen is Professor of Law and Dean of Georgetown University Law Center. Her scholarship has been concerned largely with the rights of women and children in research and medicine.

Thomas Grisso is Professor and Director of Forensic Training and Research at University of Massachusetts Medical Center. His primary research and scholarship has been on problems of competency to consent, forensic psychological assessment, and children in the legal process.

Cheryl Koopman is Assistant Professor of Clinical Psychology at Columbia University, and Research Scientist at the Research Foundation for Mental Hygiene, New York State Psychiatric Institute. Her research is focused on treatment and education of adolescents who are gay, at risk for AIDS, runaways, and otherwise vulnerable.

Ruth Macklin, a philosopher, is Professor in the Department of Epidemiology and Social Medicine at Albert Einstein College of Medicine. Her scholarship in ethical dilemmas in medicine and research has focused on a range of philosophical and bioethical issues, with considerable emphasis on the rights of children, proxy consent, and paternalism.

Gary B. Melton is Carl Adolph Happold Professor of Psychology and Law at the University of Nebraska-Lincoln, where he is also Director of the Center on Children, Families and the Law, and Director of the Law/Psychology Program. He is a community psychologist whose research and scholarship are focused largely on the rights and protection of children in research, the courts, and society.

Mary Jane Rotheram-Borus is Associate Professor of Clinical Psychology, Columbia University, Division of Child Psychiatry. Her research focus has been on children, with emphasis on stress, suicide, runaways, gay youth, and risk for AIDS in adolescents.

Joan E. Sieber is Professor of Psychology at California State University, Hayward. The focus of her scholarship and research has been ethical decision-making processes in social research, problems of studying the vulnerable and powerful, and data sharing by social scientists.

Barbara Stanley is Professor of Psychology, City University of New York/John Jay College, and Lecturer, Department of Psychiatry, Columbia University College of Physicians & Surgeons. Her research and scholarship have focused on issues of informed consent and competency, with special attention to research on youth, the elderly, and the mentally incompetent.

Ross A. Thompson is Associate Professor of Psychology, University of Nebraska. His area of research is child development, with emphasis on the social and emotional development of children, parent-infant attachment, and early socialization. He also studies psychological issues concerning children and families, including child custody, child maltreatment, and grandparents' rights..

Alexander J. Tymchuk is Associate Professor, Department of Psychiatry, the University of California, Los Angeles. His research and clinical activity have focused primarily on mental retardation, behavior modification, and informed consent.

Printed in the United States
25337LVS00002B/18

9 780803 943346